ALMOST LIKE A PROFESSIONAL

MY LIFE AND CAREER
AS A WEST TEXAS MUSICIAN

By
Cary C. Banks

Cover photo courtesy Maines Brothers Collection

James Stoddard, editor

Amanda Sneed, graphic designer
Hartsfield Design

Copyright © 2019 by Cary C. Banks. All rights reserved, including the right to reproduce this book, or portions thereof, in any form.

Visit www.carycbanks.com to learn more about the author.

First Printing: October 2019

10 9 8 7 6 5 4 3 2 1

For my beautiful and precious family.
You are my soul and my heart's inspiration,
And the reason I am blessed beyond measure.

CONTENTS

Almost Like a Professional   9

PART ONE: IN THE BEGINNING

We Had a Key	13
The Cops, the Barracuda, the Fuzz Tone, and the Mexican gang	16
Anderson Music Company	19
The Border Brass	20
You Bend Them Wires Pretty Good Son, But . . .	24
1969: It Was the Best of Times, It Was the Worst of Times	26

PART TWO: FROM HYMNALS TO HONKY TONKS

The '70's	35
26th and Boston, Part 2	42
Nashville, Part II	45
Free whiskey in the Methodist Church	48
Pandemonium at the Silver Bullet Lounge	50
I Don't Think Hank Done It This Way	52
That's Another Not-So-Funny Story	54
That'll Be a Hundred and Fifty Exposures, Please	55

PART THREE: HEY, BO DIDDLEY

Just Don't Step on My Vocals	59
West Texas Opry	61
. . . And Then the Midget Sang	62
Mr. Soul and the Infamous Cotton Club Incident	65

PART FOUR: THE MAINES BROTHERS BAND

A Honky Tonk Piano Man in a Rockin' Little Country Band	71
When 'er You Guys Gonna Go Perfeshnul?	74
Cold Water Country	75
The Record Deal	79
The Loneliness of the Heartbroken Songwriter	86
The Songs: Part One	88
All We Got is Dr Pepper	101
All the Money in My Life	101
Are We About to Have an Attitude Contest Here?	103
Don't Shoot Me, I'm Just the Bass Player	105
Dude . . . It's Just a Telethon	106
Man, This is Not an Arrangement	108
Cascade and Dog Food	109
How Long's It Take You to Pack Up 'em Drums, Anyway?	111
Gun Control	111
Singin' in a Choir with Tony Dorsett and Olive Oyl	113
The Texas Connection and the Cussin' Songs	116
Holding Country Music in My Arms	117
When He Came to Himself	120

PART FIVE: THE ONLY MOUNTAIN IN LUBBOCK

The Only Mountain in Lubbock	127
The Songs: Part II	130
MacArthur Park	139
The West Texas Music Hour is on the Air	141
The Voice	144
Oh Look . . . Tanya Tucker!	146

PART SIX: A LITTLE OL' COLLEGE WITH A GREAT BIG SOUND

The Little Ol' College with the Great Big Sound	151
That's Why They're Here	154
Faster Than I Can Listen	156
My Mama Says I Sang Them Fast Songs Purty Good	158
Welcome to the Show	159
That's the Ones We Like	160
Looking for a Drummer	161
It's Lonely at the Top	162
Moments to Remember	167
Esteemed Alums	168
Teaching the Teachers	171

PART SEVEN: FURTHER ON UP THE ROAD

Co-writers	175
Collaborations	180
Baseball Fever	182
I Wanna Be That Guy: Steve "Gittar" Williams	184
Fifteen Seconds of Film Fame	186
Opening Act	188
Gear Heads	190
Old Guy Rock	192
Hard Country, Great Music	195
It's a Family Affair	197
On Stage	207
Backstage	211
Encore	213
Acknowledgements	214

ALMOST LIKE A PROFESSIONAL

My wife's cousin, Dan Jordan, passed away several years ago. His two daughters, Jo Anna and Stephanie, are roughly the same age as my children, Katie and Cody, and we enjoyed many wonderful family gatherings together. I would always bring my guitar and sing at our Christmas gatherings. One particular Christmas, Dan brought his tuba and played along on some of the carols. Dan was very intelligent, a little shy, and always seemed to be a picture of health. I guess that's why we were all so shocked when he was diagnosed with cancer and passed away within a few short months. His wife, Pat, had let me know that one of Dan's last requests was that I sing at his funeral. He had requested the song "On the Far Side Banks of Jordan," made popular by Johnny and June Carter Cash. I'm not sure if Dan realized that particular song contains the surnames of both our families, but knowing his wry and unique sense of humor, he probably did.

The service was a positive, loving celebration of his life. My wife, Carol, spoke as did Dan's mom, Betty Jordan, and some of his close friends. Most of his friends I had never met. They all told loving, humorous stories about Dan, and the service concluded with me singing "On the Far Side Banks of Jordan."

Sometime after the service, as family and friends were gathering for the traditional funeral meal, Dan's widow, Pat, thanked me profusely for being part of the celebration of his life. She said many people had approached her to say what a lovely and uplifting service it was, and that the last song was so perfect, and the guy who sang it was really good. In fact, "He was almost like a professional."

This has become the family "inside joke" on my life as an entertainer.

Life continues to remind me not to take myself too seriously. No matter how important you think you are, God will always find little ways to keep you humble.

part one

IN THE BEGINNING

"Precious memories,

how they linger.

How they ever flood my soul."

- J. B. F. Wright

WE HAD A KEY

Those of us who grew up attending fundamentalist Christian churches can relate to the old adage about church attendance, that "We were there every time the doors were open." My dad was an elder in the Church Of Christ, my mom was an elder's wife, and we were elder's children. Not only were we there every time the doors were open, "we had a key." That meant we attended every Sunday morning, Sunday evening, and Wednesday Night Bible Study; and—at least twice a year—a week long, every night 7 PM Revival.

I suppose my rebellion against the church started very early. When I was only two or three years old, and staying the night with my grandmother Nancy, I somehow wandered across the street to the front of a small Baptist Church, where I was found just outside the front door yelling obscenities. I do not remember that incident, but I'm told I was dropping F bombs and S bombs and GD bombs like a drunken sailor. Where I learned all those words I have no clue, other than, possibly, my alcoholic step-grandfather. I don't ever remember hearing my dad use profanity, and rarely if ever would a curse word slip out of my mother's mouth. However, I remember growing up feeling a real sense of fascination with the power of swear words and profanity. I have struggled all my life not to use them, and to this day I try hard not to curse unless there is a damn good reason.

The Church of Christ does not allow any musical instruments in the worship service, so all worship music is sung a capella. The tradition of only using a capella singing in worship centered around a passage in Ephesians 5:19 that mentions "singing and making melody in your heart." It's interesting that for so many years the leaders of the church used that one verse to determine that no instruments should be played in worship.

I could never get any of the church leaders to explain the previous part of that same verse that says "speaking to one another in psalms, hymns, and spiritual songs." Would that include Psalm 150 where we are told to praise God in the sanctuary with trumpets, flutes, lyres and harps, stringed instruments and loud cymbals? I was usually dismissed with "that's Old Testament stuff and we are under a new covenant."

Those of us who attended small congregations became accustomed to certain truths about a capella church singing. The loudest bass singer in the congregation always sang a quarter tone sharp; the loudest soprano always sang a quarter tone flat with a vibrato so large you could drive a truck through it. Additionally, no matter what tempo the song leader started the song, the congregation would quickly drag it down at least 15 to 20 beats per minute.

I had absolutely no musical training growing up, but I had a decent ear and I really enjoyed the beautiful melodies of the classic hymns. What I didn't realize at the time was that I was also developing an ear for hearing and singing harmony. One Wednesday evening when I was about 11 or 12 years old, Bob Kiser, my dad's best friend and the church song leader, came up to me just before the service started and gave me a piece of paper with a bunch of numbers. He said, "Here. This is the song list for this evening . . . . You're leading the singing tonight." I guess I did all right, as a few years later he had me lead singing at a little church where he was the preacher. It was a task I came to dread, as I learned that leading a capella in a small church was—to quote my friend, John Hartin— "like trying to push a rope." Ironically, despite my less-than-pleasurable experiences leading in the Church Of Christ, a capella music is one of my most favorite forms of music.

THE ED SULLIVAN SHOW

After that fateful Sunday night in February 1964, when the Beatles first appeared on the Ed Sullivan TV show, everything in my universe changed. My friend, Hal Arbuckle, and I decided we'd learn the guitar, start a band, and within a few short months be rock stars. We spent hours listening to Beatles albums, singing along and playing "air guitar" long before that term was ever coined. However, Hal and I were off to a rocky start on our new mission, seeing that we were both good little Church Of Christ boys, and good little Church Of Christ boys "don't drink, don't chew and don't go with the girls that do." Furthermore, they most assuredly don't play devil-rock music in places where people might actually dance. So began my long and arduous battle. The more I studied and played music, the more I began to think this was something I wanted to do, could do, and was determined To Do. To the great consternation of my parents, I set out with fiery determination, iron will, and good old teenage defiance to prove that nothing was going to stop me from achieving my dreams.

I began to construct a wall of resentment that, with every Hell-Fire-and-Brimstone sermon, (which I felt was directed straight at me) I laid another brick. When I left home, I ran as fast and as far as I could from the church. But, that's another story altogether.

Fifty years of distance brings a humbling perspective to history. What I couldn't see then was that my folks were truly trying to protect me from a life they were sure would lead me straight to wreck and ruin. There are some precious things that I will be eternally grateful to my parents and my time in the Church Of Christ for giving me: For teaching me love and respect of the Holy Scriptures; for knowing that even in my most rebellious and hedonistic times, my mom continued to fervently pray for me.

A most treasured memory of mine is the image of my dad sitting next to me, holding his hymnal and singing the classic bass line: Life's evening sun, is sinking low, a few more days and I must go. To meet the deeds, that I have done. Where there will be, no setting sun. (From the hymn, A Golden Deed)

"Precious memories, how they linger. How they ever flood my soul." (w. J. B. F. Wright)

We had a key.

WORDS and MUSIC: William M. Golden, 1918. Public Domain.

THE COPS, THE BARRACUDA, THE FUZZ TONE, AND THE MEXICAN GANG

The first band I ever played with was called the Summits, which featured lead singer Danny Johnson, guitarists Brian Peay, Kyle McAlister and myself, and drummer Morgan (Bubba) Martin. One of our first rehearsals was on the driveway in front of my dad's shop next to our little house in Big Spring, Texas. We had run through only a few songs when the cops showed up and told us they had received noise complaints from some of our neighbors, and we had to shut it down. My little sister, Toya, who was six- years-old at the time, remembers that incident as the "coolest thing ever," and in her mind, the cops showing up gave us street cred as bona-fide Rock Stars. The Summits played our first official paying gig as the opening act before the Halloween Midnight Horror Show at the Ritz Theater. We had three guitar players playing out of two Sears amplifiers and a makeshift PA with two microphones plugged into a Fender Bassman amp. Dressed in our matching burgundy blazers and white turtleneck sweaters, we stumbled our way through a set of Beatles, Stones and Bob Dylan. We also played the ever-popular Louie, Louie. Since none of us could understand the "supposedly" nasty lyrics, Danny just made up his own words to the verses. Afterwards, several fans thanked us for singing the "real" words and they hoped we wouldn't get in trouble. We didn't get in trouble for performing the controversial song and I guess we did okay as nobody booed or threw stuff at us. I do remember thinking to myself, "Being up here on stage playing music is the single greatest thing I have ever experienced. This is all I want to do the rest of my life."

Kyle McAlister left the band, and the four of us continued to play all sorts of paying and non-paying gigs, the most memorable one being in the summer of 1966. My parents were very active members of the West Texas Antique Automobile Association. That summer WTAA decided to hold their annual Grand Ole Tour event at Big Bend National Park in far West Texas. For reasons I don't recall, we decided that the Summits should travel down there and perform for this Grand Ole Tour. Danny, Bubba, Brian, and I somehow loaded ourselves, all our equipment, and a fifth of Seagram's 7 into Brian's 1965 Plymouth Barracuda Hatchback and hit the road. We spent a miserable three and a half hours stuffed like smelly sardines in the car. Around sunset, we pulled into the little community of Pecos, Texas. We decided we'd stop there for the night. Right

Back yard party with my first band, The Summits Brian Peay, Danny Johnson, Cary Banks (Drummer, Morgan Martin not pictured) Photo courtesy - Cary Banks collection

in the middle of town, there was a lighted tennis court, and we decided we'd unload all our gear and perform an impromptu concert right there on the court. Brian had just acquired a Fuzz Tone guitar effects pedal and I guess we just couldn't wait to break it out to play the famous guitar lick on the Rolling Stones' song, Satisfaction. It was dark by the time we got started and by the second song, neighborhood kids were swarming the tennis courts. We were extremely excited to see a handful of teenage girls dancing to the music. Once again, we had only played a handful of songs when the cops showed up and told us we had to stop. We were bummed as the teenage girls quickly disappeared. However, one cute girl named Gloria, who lived across the street, took a shine to Danny and invited him over to her house. He actually kept in touch with her for awhile after our gig. Her parents liked Danny because he didn't try any "funny business" with their daughter. That was the first of many times I would experience the time-honored cliché, "Girls always go for the lead singer."

> *That was the first of many times I would experience the time-honored cliché, "Girls always go for the lead singer."*

As we were packing up the gear, we noticed a gang of five Mexican guys dressed in baggy pants and white, wife beater t-shirts, making their way out of the darkness toward us. Morgan began handing us parts of his drum stands and whispering, "Guys, these are the only weapons we've got." We assumed this gang was about to beat us and try to steal our equipment. As we nervously assumed some pitiful white-boy macho stances and made ready to rumble, one of the gang spoke up. "Man, how you get that geetar sound on that Satisfachun song? Eet sounds really good." It turns out the guys had a band and wanted to check out our equipment, especially the Fuzz Tone pedal.

I learned some valuable lessons that night. When you make prejudicial racial judgements, you always end up looking foolish; music transcends every race, color, and creed. And, if you're foolish enough to mix Seagram's 7 and Fresca, you deserve the wretched hangover that surely follows.

We arrived the next day at the Grand Ole Tour camping facilities and played an impromptu concert for the Antique Auto Club members and families. The kids loved us and the parents complained we were too loud. When the evening festivities were finished, we should have been more diligent in finding a flat piece of ground to bed down in our sleeping bags. We were in the middle of the West Texas desert with nothing but campfire light, while dozens of antique automobiles drove willy-nilly through the camp in the dark. One car barely missed our sleeping bags. Luckily, the driver was alert and managed to maneuver safely around a bunch of sleeping musicians.

All in all, it was a very educational experience for my first road trip gig.

ANDERSON MUSIC COMPANY

During High School, I worked afternoons, Saturdays, and summers at Anderson Music Company on Main Street in Big Spring. I wore a tie every day, showed up on time, did more than I was asked, stayed later than I had to, and never complained. It was there I received on-the-job training as salesman, repairman, custodian, clerk, and guitar teacher. Mr. V. T. Anderson had started the company in 1927 and had been highly successful not only in the music instrument business, but had built a very successful radio station that later became known as KBYG. In addition to the main floor, which featured a stuffed buffalo head above the cash register where we did all the business, the store had a basement that housed thousands of 78 RPM records, hundreds of radio and amplifier tubes, and broadcast paraphernalia. The most fascinating part of the building was the attic where Mr. Anderson had stored incredible antique and exotic instruments, including an original 1930's Rickenbacker electric guitar. By the mid sixties, his health began to fail, largely due to his chronic struggle with alcoholism. He was a kind, generous man. His wife, Billie, was a sweet, hospitable woman, who I learned to tread lightly around, never mentioning the dozens of half-empty whiskey bottles I consistently found in various hiding places around the store.

I had only been playing guitar a couple of years when I started working there, but Mr. Anderson decided we needed to offer guitar lessons with me as the new teacher. I had zero experience teaching, but he was the boss, so I got the "Mel Bay Guitar Book #1" and tried to stay at least one lesson ahead of my students.

Over the many years that Anderson Music had been in business, Mr. Anderson had worked with, booked, and befriended many musicians, including Lawrence Welk, Sonny James, and countless West Texas singers and players. I heard stories about how up-and-coming star Lefty Frizell—who played the legendary Yells Inn Bar in Big Spring where my Grandmother Nancy was a waitress—was sometimes so broke Mr. Anderson had to sell him guitar strings on credit.

He once handed me a contract dated April 1955, where he had booked a package show for the Municipal Auditorium in Big Spring, including young artists Elvis Presley, Dub Dickerson, Chuck Lee, and Gene Kay. He had booked the show for a 60%-40% split of the door, with him getting the 60%. A long line of screaming teenage girls stood outside the stage door of the Municipal Auditorium hoping to meet the rising young superstar, Elvis. My Aunt Eleanor was at that show and got not only a glimpse of him, but a touch and an autograph on her arm. To this day, she recounts the story with a giddy laugh. It wasn't long after that when Elvis first appeared on the Ed Sullivan show. Mr. Anderson would smile and say, "I never got to book Elvis again."

THE BORDER BRASS

In the fall of 1965, my sophomore year of high school, our family moved to a small community about seven miles outside of Big Spring, Texas called Sand Springs. Our new house, along with a couple of others, set above a little creek on a gravel road, just off of Interstate 20. The road was eventually paved and named Banks Road. My younger siblings and I started a new school in another little town, three miles down the road, called Coahoma. My government teacher and football coach at Coahoma High School was the legendary Spike Dykes. He had taken this ragtag little high school team from continual losing seasons to the regional playoffs. The team and Coach Dykes were given a huge article and photo

The Border Brass, Cary Banks, Tommy Rutledge, Tim Whittington, Andy Wilson, Marvin Wright, Gene Snow and David Crawford at the Fender Musical Instruments Battle of the Bands, Dallas Texas
Photo courtesy- Cary Banks Collection

spread in Life Magazine. He was actually a very good teacher, as well as a phenomenally successful coach, who would later become head coach at Texas Tech University.

Coahoma, Texas was football country, and because I enrolled late in the semester, I was the new kid in town, wasn't part of the football team, and didn't fit the mold at this small-town school. For the first few weeks, I was viewed with much skepticism—that is—until someone heard that I played guitar in a rock band. When I was asked to play an impromptu Christmas party in the school cafeteria, dressed in my Greek Fisherman's cap and Beatle Boots, crooning Sonny and Cher's big hit I Got You Babe, and the Beatles' I Saw Her Standing There, suddenly, I was everybody's friend.

I joined the school band, and because I didn't play a brass or woodwind instrument, the band director put me in the drum section. Since I had no experience playing drums, and there was no place for an electric guitar in the marching band, I was given the job of carrying the bass drum. The music program at the school was meager, to say the least. The marching band consisted of seventh and eighth graders, as well as high schoolers, and even at that, we could barely muster enough students to march up and down the field during half-time at the football games. Nevertheless, I jumped into the band scene with both feet, gave it my best shot, and began, by osmosis, to learn to read music. A couple of years later, I would actually be named to the All District Band and given the John Philip Sousa Outstanding Bandsman Award.

One of the most popular acts in the world during the mid-sixties was Herb Alpert and the Tijuana Brass. It occurred to some of us in the band that we had all the right instruments to form our own little Tijuana brass-style combo: Two trumpets, trombone, bass, drums, piano, and guitar. We began meeting in the band hall after marching practice and making our own arrangements of Herb Alpert songs. We named ourselves The Border Brass, and the next thing we knew we were booked to play a school assembly. Andy Wilson and Marvin Wright played trumpets; David Crawford played trombone and marimba, but was also a fabulous piano player; Tim Whittington played piano; Gene Snow was on the bass and Tommy Rutledge was our drummer.

Andy's dad was superintendent of the entire K-12 school complex and somehow Andy convinced him that the school needed to buy us a full-sized marimba, which The Border Brass band immediately hijacked to use in our shows. David, who already had years of keyboard experience, became quite adept at the instrument. As an added showbiz element, David, Tim, and I would all play together on the marimba, Tim playing the bass part, me in the middle playing chord rhythm, and David on the high end playing the melody.

The Border Brass became very popular around the West Texas area and soon were playing every school assembly, supermarket opening, beauty pageant, and telethon and talent contest from Ackerly to Wink. Our moms hand-sewed all our purple-and-gold matching jackets with gold cumberbunds, and our dads graciously lent us their pickups and station wagons to tote our gear around. Performing for the March Of Dimes Telethons, we got our first taste of rubbing shoulders with celebrities like Fess Parker (Disney's Davey Crockett) and Ken Berry (TV's F Troop). We discovered that at every major event where we performed, there was always some hustler trying to convince us he could make us superstars. One even tried to assure us he could get us on the Ed Sullivan show. Fortunately, our dads had pretty good BS detectors, and we never signed any shady contracts.

We landed a wonderful opportunity to be part of The Fender Musical Instruments Battle of the Bands at the 1968 Teen State Fair at the Fair Grounds in Dallas in the summer of 1968. The contest went on for four weeks and had 89 bands competing. We made the cut and were one of ten bands asked to play the final weekend competition, where we took second place. The Fender reps told us we were the best group, and even though we played several styles of music, including blues, Top 40 pop, rock, and swing, they felt they had to give first place trophy to a rock band, since it wouldn't have been good marketing to award it to a trumpet-led group. Just getting invited to participate in the contest convinced us we were rock stars and, as such, we should act like stars. Andy's dad, our lone chaperone, had booked us into a less-than-five-star hotel in a seedy part of Dallas close to the State Fairgrounds. The first night there we somehow cajoled an old drunk to buy a fifth of Jack Daniels and a quart of Smirnoff Vodka for us at a liquor store down the street from the motel. It was a pretty expensive venture, as we had to give him enough money to buy his own bottle of hooch as well. We had barely made it back to our rooms when Mr. Wilson almost caught us with the booze. We somehow managed to hide the Jack Daniels in the toilet tank and threw the vodka out the bathroom window into some bushes below.

> *Just getting invited to participate in the contest convinced us we were rock stars and, as such, we should act like stars.*

As fate would have it, when we were asked to come back for the final week end of the contest, we managed to get booked into the same room we had the previous weekend. The bottle of Jack was still in the toilet tank, and we scrounged around in the bushes and found the vodka.

After the contest, we snuck over to the park across the street in the middle of the night and got drunk together. I played my guitar and we sang Beatle's songs till the wee hours of the morning.

We played a few more gigs that summer, including big events at the University of Texas in Austin; and there was talk of a tour sponsored by Pepsi. However, when September rolled around David Crawford and I left to enroll in our respective colleges, making The Border Brass Band essentially history. We met several years later for a brief reunion dinner at a Mexican food restaurant in Midland, Texas; and despite several valiant efforts by Marvin Wright, all hope for a musical reunion faded forever when David Crawford passed away in 2014.

There are rumors that recordings of the group still exist but, as of now, their whereabouts are unknown. Marvin Wright has had a successful career in the oil business and his son, Kristopher, and daughter, Katie, were students of mine at South Plains College. Tim Whittington earned a PhD in English from Texas Tech University. Gene Snow became an award winning country singer and songwriter. Andy Wilson and Tommy Rutledge eventually moved on from music to new career and life paths.

The excitement and fun times of The Border Brass Band from Coahoma, Texas lives on in the memories of its members and many loyal fans.

YOU BEND THEM WIRES PRETTY GOOD SON, BUT . . .

My marching/concert band experience at Coahoma High was one of the most important and informative time of my life, and introduced me to a few young men who would become lifelong friends. Among them was an incredibly talented young man named Jody Nix. Jody is the son of legendary Western Swing band leader, Hoyle Nix. Hoyle had written a pretty big regional hit with the song that would later be dubbed the West Texas National Anthem: Big Ball's in Cowtown. In my life at that time, Hoyle was the only professional musician and celebrity I had ever met, and I was impressed that Jody was already a professional himself, playing drums in his dad's band. Jody also played drums in the school band, where he and I became friends. I would bring my guitar to school some days and we would jam after class in the band hall. At Jody's insistence, I got an invitation to audition for Hoyle Nix and the West Texas Cowboys. I nervously drove out to Hoyle's famous dance hall called the Stampede, just north of Big Spring. The band set up and Jody asked if Hoyle would let us jam-out on a song. I cranked up my amp and let loose with my version of Johnny Be Goode. Jody was excited by my performance and the way I played those Chuck Berry licks, bending the strings in my clumsy blues style.

> *"You bend them wires pretty good son, but you got to learn your chords."*

I could tell that Hoyle was not that impressed. After Jody and I finished our little rock and roll romp, Hoyle just smiled and suggested I join him and the band in one of their tunes. I was clueless about Western Swing Music, especially the stylistic intricacies of such guitar greats as Eldon Shamblin. Western Swing guitar borrowed from jazz-guitar stylings that basically played a different chord voicing every couple of beats, creating a moving alto line of chords and figured bass notes. I fumbled my way through the song and when it was over, Hoyle just looked at me and said, "You bend them wires pretty good son, but you got to learn your chords." I obviously didn't get the gig, (I think Hoyle was just humoring Jody to even let me audition) but that one comment set me on a lifelong journey of learning and loving to play the multitude of wonderful and beautiful chord voicings of the six string guitar.

Years later, I read an interview with Eldon Shamblin in a music magazine. The interviewer asked Eldon how many chord voicings there are on the guitar?

Eldon said, "About five thousand."

The interviewer then asked, "How many of those do you know?"

Eldon replied, "About five thousand."

Jody would later move from behind the drums to become front man, fiddler, and lead vocalist of the Texas Cowboys. In the early 1970's, his vocal performance of When You Leave Amarillo was a featured part of the highly-acclaimed, Grammy-winning album: Bob Wills, The Last Time Around. Over the years, Jody has become a highly successful and popular performer, featured on Asleep At The Wheel's Tribute to the Music of Bob

Wills album, and part of the cast of the stage play Ride with Bob, produced by Ray Benson. He continues to sing and fiddle all over Texas and still operates and performs regularly at the legendary Stampede.

1969: IT WAS THE BEST OF TIMES, IT WAS THE WORST OF TIMES

1969 was an eventful and momentous year in so many ways. It was the year man first walked on the moon, and the year three-hundred thousand young music fans gathered at a farm in upstate New York for three days of what would become a defining moment in pop music history: Woodstock.

For me it was the Year of Living Dangerously, The Good the Bad and The Ugly, and Losing My Religion.

LCC

My roommate at Lubbock Christian College, Kelly, and I started off February with the flu, the worst case of it I had ever experienced. I stayed in bed, didn't eat, and didn't hardly drink anything for a week. Only my friend, Bob Patterson, and my next door dorm-mate, Roy Gonzales, even bothered to check on me. My parents found out a week or so later and drove the whole family to Lubbock to see if I was all right; and to clean our filthy dorm room and give the dorm supervisors an earful about neglecting to see about their boy-child.

THE CHASE

Roy "Speedy" Gonzales was one crazy, horny, fun-loving Mexican (his words). He lived with his grandparents in Brownfield, Texas and decided one Friday that Kelly and I should accompany him to dinner there. His grandmother made the best homemade tortillas ever, and later that evening Roy's cousin came by and talked us into going to a big dance in Hobbs, New Mexico, a couple of hours drive from Brownfield. When we got there Kelly and I were the only two white guys in sight. Roy coaxed us into going inside, where the folks at the dance seemed less than welcoming to a couple of nervous gringos.

Nonetheless, I was really enjoying the Cajunto Band, but Kelly thought it would be best if we waited for Roy in the car. We were in the parking lot with a couple of Roy's friends when another of his cousins staggered to the car holding his bleeding stomach. He had been stabbed by a rival gang member.

The next thing I knew, Kelly and I, and several of Roy's friends and cousins were piled into a '57 Chevy, screaming a hundred miles per hour through the streets of Hobbs. "There they are!" someone shouted, and we began chasing the rival-gang Pontiac, running red lights and turning corners on two wheels.

Suddenly, the other car pulled into an alleyway with us right on its tail. The Pontiac stopped, and the driver emerged from the car pointing a shotgun at us. Somehow, Kelly and I had wound up in the front seat and—at that moment—we managed to wedge our bodies down in the floorboard.

A few months before, I had decided I didn't much need God and was going to go my own way with or without His approval. However, there in the floorboard, I briefly found my religion and whispered a desperate prayer.

> *However, there in the floorboard, I briefly found my religion and whispered a desperate prayer.*

"Lord, please don't let me die in Hobbs, New Mexico." Our driver slammed the car in reverse, putting the pedal to the metal before gunfire could break out.

Later, on the drive back home, Roy was laughing, "I never seen two white guys so scared in my life. Man! That was funny."

"No!" I yelled back. "Having a shotgun pointed at your head by a mad Mexican is not funny!"

He only laughed harder, but he had such a crazy, happy personality and mischievous Latin smile, I couldn't stay mad at him. Sadly, a couple of years later, he was killed in a car accident not far from my where my folks lived.

FLUNKIN' BAND

Aside from my friends in the dorm, the spring semester at LCC was pretty miserable. It was one of those extra-cold-and-windy, dirt-filled springs in West Texas, and the only place I felt happy was in the piano practice rooms. I missed a lot of classes just to spend more time on the piano, writing songs or trying to figure out the chord progression of the latest Glen Campbell tune written by Jimmy Webb. I was awarded a well-earned D in Band that semester. I had a bad attitude about life in general and school in specific. However, there were a couple of "goods" that semester. I was a member of the Men's Social Organization, Koinonia," and members of the group acted out a skit as I sang the Beatles' song Rocky Raccoon at the annual Master Follies event. Our performance won first-place in the contest. I barely passed my other classes, but scored an A on my final in Theory and Composition class with a little piece entitled Song Man. My friend, Bob Patterson, and I celebrated the end of the school year by taking my 1965 Corvair down to Padre Island in South Texas and spending a couple of weeks camped-out on the beach. Bob was one of those true friends who would call me out on my boorish behavior. He also had a beautiful Martin acoustic guitar that he let me play. Ironically, it was at a Christian school where I first began to lose my religion. I can't really lay the blame on the institution; I was headed that direction anyway.

LOSIN' MY RELIGION AND OTHER THINGS

Along with losin' my religion that summer, I lost my virginity. I learned some hard lessons from that experience. Among them was: liquor plus raging hormones always equals bad judgement; and just because you do the deed doesn't mean she thinks you're all that. It was quite a rude awakening for me when she showed complete disinterest in the days and weeks following our little tryst. To her credit, I wouldn't have wanted to be around me back then, either. That certainly wasn't the first or last time I would experience rejection from the opposite sex. I came to expect it and in many cases, I had certainly earned it.

UNCLE SAM CALLING

I tried school again in the fall at the local Howard County Junior College, but lasted only a few weeks. The day I dropped out, I drove straight down to the local Army recruiter and joined up. Although my dad had served proudly in the army in occupied Japan in World War II, he and my mom were not happy with my decision. The Vietnam War, with all its horror, invaded the households of millions of Americans every evening on the nightly TV news. One of their closest couple friends at church had lost a child in that bloody conflict, and my parents were not immune to the fear that their first-born son could be sent to that far-off land of death and destruction. Nevertheless, this was 1969 and if you were a poor boy in West Texas and had just surrendered your college deferment, you were as good as drafted anyway. My one hope was that my guitar abilities might somehow land me an audition and a place in one of the army bands.

A few days later, I found myself standing naked in a freezing-cold room in an Army Recruitment Center in Sweetwater, Texas with dozens of other frightened young fellows suffering the utter humiliation of an army physical. "Bend over, turn your head and cough, wipe that smile off your face, sit down, shut up, and fill out these forms" were just some of the orders barked into our ears over the next several hours. I looked around the room and knew, just from statistics broadcast on the nightly news, that many of these young men wouldn't live to see their twenty-first birthday. A feeling of melancholy like I had never known washed over, under, and through my soul. Sometime later, toward the end of the exam, I was directed to a young intern who would check my hearing. As a toddler, I had developed a bad ear infection resulting in a surgical procedure to clean and heal the damaged mastoid bone behind my left ear. The intern began the examination by looking in that ear, then excused himself and brought back the head doctor, who proceeded to examine both my ears intently and repeatedly. After a few moments of consultation with one of the other doctors, he came back into the room and said, "Son, the fluid in your ears is cloudy and dark, you have perforations in both eardrums, and you are not fit for military service." He signed a few forms, and the next thing I knew I was on a bus back home with a 1Y medical deferment. Little did I know the profound ramifications that medical exam would have on my life and hearing, forty years later. All the way home, I pondered what my next move would be. I knew I wanted to be a professional musician and songwriter, but I had no clue where to go next.

| NASHVILLE, PART ONE |

My friend, Mike Colclazer, played in a band with a talented young man named Steve Holley. Steve was ambitious, proud of his abilities, and sure he was going to be a star. In a whirlwind of events, he married his young sweetheart, Judy, whose brother, Danny Lane, was playing drums for rising country star Jeannie C. Riley, whose recording of Harper Valley PTA had sold millions of records. Steve and I had written a couple of songs together, and virtually overnight he decided that he and Judy and I should pack our stuff—including his drums and my guitar and amp—into my little '65 Corvair, and move to Nashville.

A very influential doctor in Big Spring had gone into partnership with a local musician/songwriter/celebrity named Ben Hall to open a recording studio in Nashville. I had watched Ben Hall and The Circle 4 Ramblers on their Saturday afternoon country music TV show, and knew he had a connection with Buddy Holly, and that his steel guitar player, Weldon Myrick, was becoming a well-established studio musician there. When we arrived in Nashville, we somehow finagled a tour of Mr. Hall's studio, where Steve informed him that we were the latest, greatest thing to show up in Nashville, and were on the verge of setting the music industry on fire. Mr. Hall was gracious, but I could tell he wasn't impressed with the bluster, even if we were from Big Spring. After a brief tour of the facility, he politely showed us the exit with the non-spoken implication to not let the door hit us in the butt on the way out.

Judy's brother, Danny, and his wife, Sally (Townes), who was a talented musician as well, were staying at a hippie haven just outside Nashville with several other musicians, girlfriends, and groupies. Steve decided we should take up residence there as well. There I had my first, and only, LSD experience, freaking out and wandering around in a paranoid state for the next couple of days. Within the week we decided Nashville wasn't ready for our talents so we headed north to Milwaukee, Wisconsin to stay with Steve's grandmother and aunt. In Milwaukee, besides nearly freezing to death, we lived in a rundown tenement and almost got knifed in a local diner. When the snow cleared enough for us to leave, we were out of money so we headed back to West Texas.

In my mind, I was young and cool, pretty good on the guitar, and had this burning desire to be a famous singer songwriter. In reality, I was young, inexperienced, totally unprepared, and basically didn't know nuthin' 'bout nuthin'. My first ugly truth lesson about Nashville was that nobody had sent for me, nobody knew I was there, and nobody cared when I left.

> *My first ugly truth lesson about Nashville was that nobody had sent for me, nobody knew I was there, and nobody cared when I left.*

In the fall of 1969, I had left the halls of higher learning and enrolled in the University Of Hard Knocks. For the next two decades of hopeful highs and despairing lows, I would labor to earn a PhD in how to survive and avoid being roadkill on that lost highway called the music business.

part two

FROM HYMNALS TO HONKY-TONKS

"Your arm's too short

to box with God."

- James Weldon Johnson

THE '70'S

"How did a good little Church Of Christ boy wind up playing music in a honky-tonk bar?"

By the early 1970's, the Beatles had broken up, Janis Joplin, Jimi Hendrix, and Jim Morrison had all died of drug overdoses, and a group of drug-crazed hippies led by Charles Manson had committed a string of gruesome and highly-publicized murders in California. The Vietnam War was becoming more and more controversial, leading to mass protests across the country. When four peaceful students at Kent State University were killed by National Guard troops, the Age of Aquarius with its dreams of peace, love, and flower power quickly began to wither.

26TH AND BOSTON, PART 1

Following my first disastrous trip to Nashville, I slinked back to Texas, my tail between my legs. A few weeks after, driving too fast in an automobile deemed "unsafe at any speed," I managed to run my '65 Corvair into an unforgiving guardrail. I found myself with no car, no job, no money, and no prospects. With only my guitars, one change of clothes, and four dollars in my pocket, I decided to try Lubbock again. I hitched a ride with Danny Johnson, and I happened to walk into Jent's House of Music and saw my friend, Van Stansell, whom I'd met while we were both attending Lubbock Christian College (Now Lubbock Christian University). Van was repairing instruments at the store and immediately talked Mr. Jent into hiring me as a guitar teacher/salesman. He and I became roommates and rented a tiny little house at 26th and Akron Street, a few blocks from the music store. It had one small room that housed a bed, a spinet piano Van had talked Mr. Jent into letting us borrow, Van's stereo, and my guitar and amp. A tiny kitchen and bath filled out the remainder of our hovel.

Just around the corner at 26th and Boston was a convenience store where we bought cigarettes, Dr Peppers, and Playboy magazines. Across the street was a dry cleaners, a few small shops, and a neighborhood post office. I am told a drugstore once occupied one corner, its parking lot a popular after-hours hangout for local teenagers, who parked their cars and tuned their radios to KWKH out of Shreveport, Louisiana. Among the young people listening and dancing to the radio at that infamous lot was a young musician named Buddy Holly. The location's proximity to Texas Tech University made it a popular spot for college students as well.

Just about sunset, on May 11, 1970, Van and I were in the house trying to write some new music when the weather turned strange. It suddenly got very warm and still. It felt like all the oxygen had been sucked out of the atmosphere. We went outside and saw the weirdest-looking clouds I'd ever seen. We didn't own a TV, and for some reason the sole radio in the house would only pick up static.

We felt the wind rising like crazy, and it began to thunder and lightning, and rain louder and harder than I had ever remembered. All the electricity in the house went off, and we were left sitting in the dark wondering what the hell was going on. Police cars, fire trucks, and ambulances filled the streets, and the sounds of sirens blasted all night long. When I got up the next morning, I wandered outside to see not one leaf left on a single tree in the neighborhood. The street was littered with leaves, branches, and all kinds of debris, and the sirens still pierced the air.

Van and I went to work, and people were milling around, some looking bewildered and anxious while others were downright panicked. We didn't realize a major tornado had struck Lubbock, leaving dozens dead and injured, and destroying a two-mile-wide swath of homes, businesses, and lives. In fact, it had touched down and destroyed a major portion of Jones Stadium at Texas Tech University, a little over a mile away from our house. The city of Lubbock was virtually shut down for the next week, and water and electricity wasn't restored to a large portion of the town for several days. Relatives of the Jent family, who lived in Kansas, were mortified when they attempted to call Mr. and Mrs. Jent the next day and were informed by the telephone operator that "due to a tornado, Lubbock, Texas no longer exists." Fortunately, the Jent's were able to contact relatives soon after to let them know they were safe; and yes, Lubbock, Texas was still on the map. I would learn a few years later that my friend and mentor, Bud Andrews, was working the night shift at KFYO radio in downtown Lubbock the night of the tornado, and had remained on the air as the mighty storm blew right over the building where he was broadcasting. He would receive recognition and an award from the President of the United States for his bravery and faithfulness to the people of Lubbock and the surrounding areas.

JENT'S HOUSE OF MUSIC

I worked at Jent's House of Music, teaching guitar, selling instruments and sheet music, and moving pianos. I learned a lot about the retail music business and the intricate and sometimes disturbing psychological complexities of working in a family-owned business, which included Papa Ray and Mama Mickie Jent, two daughters, Karen and Vicky, and

A favorite gathering place for Lubbock musicians
Photo courtesy - Karen Jent Pollard

son-in-law, Gene. I loved the Jent family, and they were always kind, supportive, encouraging, and very generous to me. However, it didn't take long to learn that Rule Number One was Mama Jent was always right; and Rule Number Two was never challenge Rule Number One. My time at Jent's afforded me many opportunities to meet and interact with so many great musicians in the community, and gave my band a place for after-hours rehearsals. Another added bonus was Mama Jent was a good cook, and I enjoyed many a great meal at their house. There were many times that I played music just on the chance that someone might feed me. I got good enough that I rarely missed a meal.

| PAYBACK'S A BITCH |

One of the most memorable characters I met while working at Jent's House of Music was an organ salesman named R. C. Matheny. R. C. sang in some country bands in various clubs around town and, unfortunately, fought a lifelong battle with the bottle. Many was the morning R. C. would stumble into the store, hung over and looking like nine miles of bad road. Of course, a couple of us young guys working there couldn't resist the sadistic temptation to bang on cymbals, turn electric guitar amps up to 11, and whack away on some ungodly loud guitar riff. We thought it was big fun. R. C. was not amused and would shoot us an I'll get you back for this look from his bloodshot eyes. I really liked R. C. and was mesmerized by his stories of honky-tonk debauchery. One weekend Mr. and Mrs. Jent were out of town visiting relatives and daughters, and Karen and Vicky, and son-in-law Gene were on a road trip with the Texas Tech Band. They had asked me to house-sit and feed their large pack of dogs. After work that Saturday I drove to their house and could hear the hungry dogs barking like crazy. I put the key they had given me into the front door and it would not open. I tried several more times, went around to the back door, but still had no luck. They had inadvertently given me the wrong key. The dogs were in the house and barking ever louder, so I tried the bathroom window by the side, which they sometimes left unlocked. Miraculously, it was not locked. I opened the screen, raised the window, and began crawling into the house. I was nearly in when I felt a tap on the sole of my shoe. Here I was—halfway in the house—the dogs absolutely insane by now, and I suddenly had a sinking feeling in my stomach. I wormed my way out of the window to find a policeman, nightstick in hand, asking what the hell I was doing breaking into this house. My tongue-tied attempt to tell him I was supposed to be there, that I had the wrong key and hungry dogs, fell on deaf ears. I pleaded with him to take me back to the store, praying there was somebody still there who could verify that I was an employee authorized to be at the house.

We pulled up to the parking lot in front of Jent's, and all the lights were out save one lonely bulb in the back. The front door was locked, and I began to pound furiously, hoping someone would hear. Finally, out of the back I saw my salvation in the form of R. C. Matheny slowly sauntering to the front to unlock the door. We stepped inside, and the policeman told him he had found me breaking and entering and needed to know if I was indeed an employee of Jent's House of Music. With the cool calmness of a Gary Cooper cowboy, R. C. took a long, slow draw from his cigarette, looked at me, then looked at the policeman and nonchalantly said, "Never seen him before in my life."

"Never seen him before in my life."

At that point, my already-panicked countenance turned a whiter shade of pale. It seemed like an eternity before R. C. shot me a devilish grin and confessed to the cop that I indeed worked there, and he was just having a good laugh at my expense. At that moment, I didn't know if I wanted to kiss him or kill him. I thanked him profusely and never, ever again, tortured him in the least when he came into work hungover. Many years later after R. C. had passed, I related that story to his daughter. She laughed and agreed that was indeed her dad's sense of humor.

| DALLAS |

After leaving Lubbock in early 1972, I found myself in Dallas, Texas, staying with a former bandmate, Mike Reynolds. I hung out at folk clubs and beer joints like the Rubiat and Poor David's Pub, listening to local artists such as Michael Martin Murphy, B. W. Stevenson, and Ray Wylie Hubbard. I booked a few coffee houses and restaurants, but wasn't making much headway in my career. I soon discovered that in most of the places I played, my attempts to sing those soft fingerpicking James Taylor ballads usually turned into guitar-banging, vocal-shouting contests, competing with breaking dishes, loud, obnoxious customers and feedback-squealing P. A.'s. I was writing like crazy, but it seemed like "the harder I tried, the worser it got."

At one point, my friend and fellow guitar player, Mike Colclazer, had moved to Dallas, and he and I had wrangled an audition with RCA Records representative, Merlin Littlefield. He liked a couple of our songs, but gave us the stock Music-Business-Executive line: "Leave your tape and we'll get back with you." We left the tape; and soon—all hope of hearing from RCA records. Years later when I met Merlin Littlefield again in his ASCAP office, I thought it wise not to bring up our previous meeting.

I was scuffling around trying to book solo gigs at restaurants and coffee houses, and book meetings with small, local music publishing companies. Mike Reynolds had a job working with his sister-in-law, Barbara, in a tractor-parts supply house. I was staying with Mike, and he and I would often take our guitars to his brother, Max's, house to serenade Barbara in hopes of earning a free meal. She always graciously obliged. I think she felt sorry for me, because she offered me a job at the supply house, where I learned to work with microfilm and run an offset printing press.

While working there was dull, lifeless, and unfulfilling, working for Barbara Reynolds was a ray of sunshine. She was a beautiful and gracious friend, who was always supportive and encouraging of my music, letting me spend hours at her house playing her piano. During the time I worked with her, she went through a messy divorce from her husband, Max. Being a single mom was a rough and lonely time, and I often babysat her young son, Mark, when she needed to get away from it all and heal her heart.

WEDDING SINGER

Mr. Weber, the owner of the tractor-parts business, had a daughter named Debbie who worked there as well. Debbie asked me to perform at her wedding and accompany her singer friend, Jana, a sorority sister of hers at Texas Tech. I played guitar and Jana and I sang the Wedding Song and Sunrise, Sunset. Jana (King Evans) was a beautiful and talented singer, and I had an instant crush on her. After she graduated from Texas Tech, she moved to Nashville and landed a spot as one of the background vocalists on the Nashville Now TV show. I would run into her again a decade later when the Maines Brothers Band performed on the show.

LOSING MY RELIGION

By the time 1973 rolled around, Mike Reynolds had pretty much surrendered any musical aspirations he had, but we both set out on a course to lose the God of Abraham, Isaac, and Jacob, and all those New Testament saints, and find our true inner selves. We dabbled in Mind Control, Transcendental Meditation, Eastern Mysticism, and practiced positive thinking and attended lectures on Buda, Krishna, Kundalini Fire, white magic, and on and on and on. I remember hours of meditation where I would chant mantras and—in my mind—hear the voice of some wise Indian Yoga Master chanting in a soft, soothing Indian accent:

"You must close your eyes, breathe deeply, let go of all your troubles and cares. Relax and release yourself from this world. Lose your will and let go of all ambition. Become One with the universe. Surrender your being to the Great Nothingness."

And that was what I found. Absolute nothingness. Later on, I recognized that this positive-thinking- create-your-own-happiness-and-bliss-philosophy that the metaphysical gurus were espousing was the same snake-oil pitch the prosperity gospel preachers were peddling. A still, small voice in the back of my mind kept reminding me of those scriptures I'd heard as a kid: Beware false prophets. I found myself in a spiritual no-man's land. I figured if I couldn't find God in Eastern religion, transcendental meditation, New Age Metaphysics, or whatever, then I would just ignore Him and make my own destiny. Better yet, I would recreate God in my own image. This prodigal son might have been up to his neck in a feces-filled pigpen, but he damn sure wasn't going to admit failure and go home. I determined that somehow, someway, music was going to be my salvation. I hadn't yet discovered the truth of the old James Weldon Johnson poem: "Your arm's too short to box with God." I would suffer several KO's before that truth sank in.

26TH AND BOSTON, PART 2

I CAN'T SING A LOVE SONG

In 1974, I moved from Dallas back to Lubbock and was working, again, at Jent's House of Music. One afternoon I was running an errand for Mr. Jent and driving down Boston Avenue. As I stopped at the intersection of Boston and 26th street, a song title jumped into my head: I can't sing a love song, without your harmony. I pulled into a small parking lot, found a leaky old ballpoint pen and a torn piece of paper, and scribbled: I can't sing a love song, without your harmony, I can't make it solo, I need you here with me. Please don't leave me lonely, for darling can't you see? I can't sing a love song, without your harmony.

I Can't Sing a Love Song Cary C. Banks © 1975 International Doorway Music ASCAP/Universal Music Group Corporation ASCAP

I finished my errand and drove as fast as I could back to the store, grabbed a guitar, and holed-up in the little teaching studio, finishing the song in about an hour. A few days later I played it for my friend and publisher, Bud Andrews, and he sent me to Don Caldwell Studios where Lloyd Maines recorded me singing a guitar/voice demo of the song. Bud and his partner, Big Ed Wilkes, had become successful in the music business producing comedy records for the legendary country comedian, Jerry Clower.

Working with Bud Andrews and Big Ed Wilkes afforded me many opportunities to learn and experience the inner workings of the record

Today at 26th and Boston
Photo courtesy - Rachel Faris Ross

---

and music publishing business. Music performance rights organizations (commonly known as PRO's) like BMI, ASCAP and SESAC collect fees from radio and television stations, theaters, restaurants and bars, etc. for the use of copyrighted music; and in turn, distribute money to music publishers and songwriters in the form of royalties. In the 1970's, these PRO's did not pay performance royalties for spoken word recordings like comedy records. Producers of comedy recordings discovered that if they had some sort of instrumental music track playing quietly underneath the voice recording, the comedy track could then be copyrighted as a musical composition and thereby qualify for royalties. Of course the underlying music bed would have to be original music. I and several of my guitar-playing friends were hired to play solo acoustic guitar on the comedy recordings. We would mostly improvise happy, up-tempo country-style picking. Our performances became part of the copyrighted musical composition that was owned by the artist and producers. We were not given any songwriting credits as we were simply contract labor session musicians. Some session players complained that our creativity was being exploited, but most of us were just glad to get the work and have our names listed on the album credits. The music we played was generally mixed so quietly that most listeners weren't even aware that there was music on the comedy records. I was fortunate to play a guitar track on Jerry Clower's single: What Christmas Means To Me." I played on several other comedy records as well.

Big Ed and Bud had fortuitously discovered a new comic artist, Jerry Jordan, from Brownfield Texas, and had produced a number one record with him called The Phone Call from God. The album had been so successful that MCA Records had asked for a follow-up record. The second record: Don't Call Me, I'll Call You, featured Jerry talking to God on the CB radio. This was the mid-1970's and the Citizens Band (CB) radio was the latest craze. The first album had featured The Phone Call from God comedy track and also had Jerry and his brother and their wives singing some gospel songs. For the new record Jerry wanted to record a song that would feature him as a solo vocalist. Bud played him my demo of I Can't Sing A Love Song, and the next thing I knew, we were in the studio recording a track that would become my first major label cut as a songwriter. After the album was released I traveled with the Jordan family all across the South and Midwest as their guitarist and piano player. I finished the tour and waited for those big royalty checks to start rolling in. I was dating a sweet girl named Lesli Bishop at the time, and when she heard the song playing on the radio she excitedly exclaimed, "You really have made it now, haven't you?" As it turned out . . . not so much. How quickly I was to be reminded of the harsh reality of the music business. The album got into the Top 30's on the Billboard charts, and though I did receive a couple of paltry royalty checks, the record died a quiet death, and MCA dropped Jerry from the label. He went back to his first love as a visual artist and painter, but I decided it was time to test Nashville again. (*See Nashville Part II*)

Today, the corner of 26th street and Boston avenue, where the convenience store once sat, is home to J & B Coffee, where friends and I sometimes meet to drink exotic coffee and talk about the music business. Across the street, where I pulled into the parking lot to write the beginning lyrics of I Can't Sing a Love Song, sits a highly successful recording studio called Amusement Park Studios, owned and operated by my good friend and colleague, Scott Faris and his lovely wife, Amy. I've been privileged to record a few tracks there myself.

I still get some tiny songwriting royalties from I Can't Sing A Love Song. Whud-a-thunk-it?

And like a vinyl record on an old turntable, my musical career turns round and round.

NASHVILLE, PART II

Traveling with Jerry Jordan and his family throughout the South and Midwest in the winter of 1976 was an eye-opening experience. We would play some tiny church way out in the sticks, and people would show up from miles around to hear The Phone Call from God. Jerry was an instant, and I must admit, very reluctant star. It seemed no matter where we went, any time day or night, when folks found out that Jerry Jordan was on-board the mobile home we were using to travel, they phoned relatives and friends, and stormed the vehicle for an autograph, a picture, or just to ooh and aah and tell their acquaintances they had met a real live celebrity. I don't think Jerry had anticipated that his comedy record would achieve the incredible success or response that it did. In just a few short months he had gone from being a full-time visual artist, specializing in oil painting, and a part-time evangelist-comedian, to having a number one record and performing on the Grand Ol' Opry. We played churches, county fairs, showcases, and anywhere two or more were gathered. I had related to Jerry my Church Of Christ background and my disdain for all things "churchy." He and his wife, Marilyn, and sister-in-law Colleen, were always gracious and tolerant of my less-than-righteous attitude about church; and when we would visit some charismatic little backwoods church where I would be assaulted with "Praise the Lord, brother; Praise the Lord, brother," Jerry would give me a wink, a smile, and a little chuckle under his breath. I also noticed that in our big showcases with well-known Southern Gospel groups, some of the band members could drink and smoke and party as hearty as any heavy metal rock group. At first I thought it hypocritical of those folks to be singing for Jesus and partying like heathens, but I eventually realized that, like all of us, the spirit is willing, but the flesh is weak. I did notice that almost all those Southern Gospel groups had talented piano players, and I learned a lot just watching and listening to them play. I found it amazing that so many of the great piano players in popular music had their beginnings in the church.

The highlight of my time with the Jordans was doing a concert with special guest, Dale Evans. As a kid growing up in Big Spring I spent many a Saturday morning glued to the television watching the Roy Rogers and Dale Evans TV show. To be performing onstage with her was something I would never have dreamed possible, but there I was playing along while she sang Happy Trails. During the tour, I met a number of music business bigwigs and even had the glorious opportunity to attend an MCA Records party in Nashville and rub shoulders with country music legends like Brenda Lee, Bill Monroe, Nat Stuckey, and a very young Tanya Tucker, who exploded into the room wearing a floor-length mink coat, sunglasses the size of grapefruits, and an ever-present entourage. I was pretty starstruck, so I mostly tried to appear cool and not embarrass myself. I did feel pretty special when Brenda Lee initiated a conversation with me. I was riding high on Jerry Jordan's coattails but I would soon be brought down to the cold, hard ground of the fickle here-today, gone-tomorrow world of music.

I was pretty starstruck, so I mostly tried to appear cool and not embarrass myself.

While on the road with the Jordan family, I happened to meet a brother and sister duo called Tim and Monica, talented kids out of Nashville, who patterned their show loosely around the style of Donnie and Marie Osmond. Their mom and keyboard accompanist, Janice, heard me performing with the Jordan family, and asked if I would join Tim and Monica onstage for the rest of the tour. She and husband, Don, invited me to Nashville to join the group as full-time guitarist, arranger, and songwriter. I thought this might be my big chance to get a foot in the door in Nashville, so I didn't think twice about packing my belongings and heading up to the BIG N.

The kids were trying to get a record deal and had booked some recording-session time with a noted producer. After cutting a few tracks of my songs, we hit the road, travelling from Alabama to Missouri, and on to Las Vegas for a gig at the Fremont Hotel Casino, where we shared the stage with Waylon Jennings' former group, The Kimberleys. We would play from 9:00-9:45 p.m. and the Kimberleys would take the stage from 10:00-10:45. We would come back at 11:00-11:45, and so on until the last band finished at 3:00 in the morning. The folks in The Kimberleys, especially the lead female vocalist, were friendly, cordial, unpretentious, and encouraging. I enjoyed getting to hang with them. Needless to say, there was a lot of downtime, filled by me with fifty-cent Johnnie Walker Black whiskey on the rocks, followed by a staggering walk back to a motel where the band stayed. It only took me losing one paycheck to learn when you're a poor musician working Vegas, you Never Gamble. When we finally made our way back to Nashville, I spent my days burning shoe-leather up and down 16th Avenue, trying to get any publisher to listen to my songs. No one was impressed that I had a cut on the Jerry Jordan album, which had quickly fallen off the charts, or that I had shared a drink and conversation with Brenda Lee.

When I did get someone to listen, I mostly heard the standard Nashville publisher response: "Thank you very . . . Next."

Tim and Monica weren't having any luck securing a recording contract, and gigs had become sparse. I was starving, out of money, and spiritually, emotionally and artistically bankrupt, so I loaded all my earthly possessions in my '69 Camaro and headed back to Texas. As I saw Nashville disappearing in my rearview mirror once again, I couldn't help but think that even though this time someone had sent for me, few cared I was leaving, and nobody would really miss me.

I limped into Arlington, Texas where my dear friend, Mary Hall, bought me a meal and spotted me gas money to get home. Dreams die hard, but they make no sound as they pass away.

FREE WHISKEY IN THE METHODIST CHURCH

Carol and I were married November 18, 1978 at the First United Methodist Church of Irving, Texas. My bride was stunningly beautiful, and I was remarkably calm considering I had spent the prior two days trying to make sure my brothers, Jake and Russ, and sister, Toya, and my two bandmates/groomsmen, Jack and Johnny, all boarded an airplane in Lubbock and arrived in Dallas on-time for the rehearsal dinner and the wedding ceremony—sober. On top of that, I had to make it all the way through the wedding facing the preacher, Reverend Earl E. Harvey, who at its conclusion would become my father-in-law.

Carol had come to Lubbock from the Dallas area to attend Texas Tech University. Later, she began working for an eye surgeon and became roommates with a young girl from Odessa named Annie Cole. Annie was dating Johnny James, my best friend, and drummer with several bands we played in together. At the time, early 1977, I was living in Nashville, but Johnny was constantly talking to Carol about his cool songwriter friend, Cary, insisting she should meet him the next time he was in Lubbock. Carol grew pretty tired of Johnny's incessant talk of me, and though she had never met me, decided she already didn't like me. When I returned to Lubbock a few months later, Johnny and Annie made it their mission to get us together. It worked. I became totally smitten with Carol. She was beautiful, smart, strong, independent, and had the sweetest, most gentle, insightful, and loving spirit of anyone I had ever met.

There was just one problem. Her Dad was a Methodist preacher and her Mom was a Methodist preacher's wife. I had spent the last ten years running as fast and far away as I could from all things church and religious. My own parents were already convinced that my life as a musician had me headed for the gates of Hell, and I sure didn't need in-laws preaching and praying my soul back into the Kingdom of Righteousness. What followed was nothing short of a miracle. Carol's folks didn't judge or condemn me, or try to convince me to give up my honky tonk musician career. They just loved me, supported me, encouraged me,

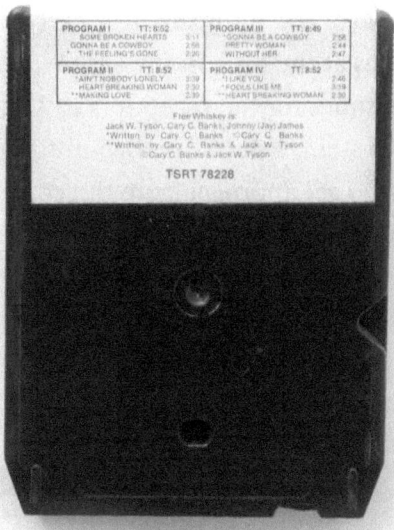

Photo design courtesy - Bob Hudnal

---

and lived out their faith before me. I would come to love, respect, and cherish them both deeply.

My mother-in-law, Vivian, and all the ladies at the Irving United Methodist church, took great pains to beautifully decorate both the sanctuary for the wedding service and the church basement for the reception. Al, the music minister, sang a song that I had written called "Till Forever." We had to change the lyrics to include the word God in order to satisfy the requirements for wedding music in the Methodist Church. I had been asked to perform as well, and sang Cat Steven's Morning Has Broken. (It was on the approved song list.) Looking back, I wish I had not agreed to sing during the service, as I felt like part of my wedding was me performing. The ceremony went beautifully, and we all adjourned to the basement for the reception. My parents and Grandmother Nancy, my brothers and sister, all of Carol's family, and most of the church were at the wedding. The church ladies had even baked a guitar-shaped chocolate cake for the groom's table.

Two of my groomsmen, Jack Tyson and Johnny James, were my bandmates at the time in the Free Whiskey Band. Earl had asked us to play a few songs for the reception and had arranged for us to use the church's PA system. I didn't realize until later that he had gone way out of his way to get approval from the church board to have the reception in the church. As it began, Earl walked to the microphone, thanked everyone for coming, and announced that the groom and his band would now sing a few songs. He then smiled and added, "This is the only time you'll have Free Whiskey in the Methodist church."

PANDEMONIUM AT THE SILVER BULLET LOUNGE

"Saturday night's all right for fighting," sang Sir Elton John. Those of us who've spent our nights working in honky-tonks, bars, dives, and nightclubs know that any given night where liquor and human emotions collide, sooner or later (generally sooner) somebody's gonna start a fight. As Lloyd Maines would say, "It's either over a bottle or a woman; most often, the latter." In my decades of performing in bars, I've seen many a fight, but one that stands out is a New Year's Eve gig at the original Bullet Bob's Silver Bullet Lounge.

My friend, Terry Creswell, and I had been performing at the Silver Bullet for several months There was a group of about three or four couples that had become regulars at our performances, and one of the young ladies was particularly adept at stirring up trouble. This particular night, she had somehow squeezed herself into a pair of low cut jeans that were way too small, and a halter top that left little to the imagination; and of course, had managed to start the tension early. Several times during the evening, shouting matches and threats could be heard above the music, and I knew from experience that tonight's gig was probably not going to end well. The yelling and posturing between this particular young lady and a couple of other girls and their husbands continued to escalate until—shortly after Auld Lang Syne and the popping of the champagne corks—a drink was spilled, a table was turned over, and pandemonium ensued.

As the chaos erupted, I recalled the warning words of my old friend and longtime western swing fiddler, Buzz James: "If a fight breaks out, don't stop playin'. That'll just piss off the crowd. Don't play nothin' too slow or too fast. Just pick you a nice medium tempo two-step song and keep playin' and lookin' for a place to hide." The Silver Bullet was a fairly small venue, and within a couple of minutes, everyone except the bartenders, waitresses, and the band was in the fray. Suddenly, from seemingly out-of- nowhere, a flying fist of fury caught the troublemaking young lady right in the kisser, sending her hurtling across the room, where she landed flat on her back like a wet bar towel—finally silent.

At that point, Terry and I looked at each other, turned off the PA system, put our guitars in the cases, and silently slipped out the back door. The bartender gave us a knowing glance and reached for the telephone to call the police. The crowd of brawlers were still hard at it and never even noticed the band was gone.

That was not even the weirdest or most violent event we experienced at the Silver Bullet Lounge.

Unfortunately, one particular Friday Night, not long after the New Year's Eve fiasco, Terry and I had just finished our last set, packed up our gear, and were headed across the parking lot to our respective vehicles. Suddenly, from out of the shadows, a big, burly cowboy jumped Terry and commenced beating him senseless, while his buddies held me down and restrained me from coming to his aid. The cowboy was furiously accusing Terry of "messin' around with his wife," and was determined to inflict as much harm as he could. Terry was innocent of the charges, but it didn't matter. The mayhem continued until someone threatened to call the police. The cowboy and his buddies quickly disappeared into the night. It was all a big misunderstanding, but the damage to Terry's body was pretty significant. After that incident, we decided we had taken our last "bullet" for that little bar, and it was time to bid it a less than fond farewell.

I DON'T THINK HANK DONE IT THIS WAY

In my many years of watching the world from a bandstand, I've seen my share of sights from the sublime to the ridiculous. I've seen couples dancing so smooth and flawless you would swear they were one body. I've seen marriage proposals; major breakups; long, wet kisses; bloody fisticuffs; and some things I will never be able to unsee.

I was playing a gig with my friend, Johnny James, at the Longhorn Saloon in East Lubbock. The bar was the quintessential honky-tonk dive, one of those joints where they frisk you for weapons, and if you don't have any, they give you one. That's an exaggeration, but not much. At the Longhorn Saloon you played classic country music that people could dance to, or you didn't play anything at all. The clientele was mostly blue-collar workers, hard-scrabble cowboys, roughnecks, and chain-smoking divorcees with skintight, gold-lamé pants, ruby-red lipstick, and electric-blue eyeshadow.

I was playing guitar that night; Johnny was drumming and doing most of the lead vocals. Our keyboard player was a precious lady named Rita "Ma" Havens. Her son, Bobby, was a well-known guitarist and songwriter with the Larry Trider Band. Terry Creswell was playing bass for us. Johnny was a handsome guy with an incredibly beautiful, soulful voice. There was never a shortage of women vying for Johnny's attention at these places, and many times they were not shy about bringing their obvious flirtations right up to the stage.

About halfway through the second set, I saw an older woman staggering her way across the dance floor. This poor lady could have been anywhere from sixty-five to a hundred and five years old, and was so skinny she would have to run around in the shower to get wet. She was also so drunk it was a wonder she could stand, much less walk. The few teeth she still had were miraculously holding the cigarette that was dangling from her weathered lips. It was pretty obvious she was making a beeline for the drums.

Right there in front of Johnny, she starts dancing, slobbering some incoherent babble that sounds something like "Come and git it, baby."

She then proceeds to start performing the most bizarre striptease in the history of the world. She almost has her shirt completely off, when Johnny—who is right in the middle of singing Waylon Jennings' big hit, I Don't Think Hank Done It This Way—starts yelling into the mic for the bar manager to come get this crazy woman before she bares it all. The manager is laughing his butt off, while we're trying our best to keep the song going and maintain some kind of professional demeanors.

The dancers were mildly amused, but mostly unfazed by the crazy strip show, until the poor lady fell into the drums. The manager and the bartender finally wrestled her off the stage and back to a table. Despite her drunken protestations about just wanting to party with "that drummer boy," they somehow kept her at bay while they called for a cab to take her home.

As I watched this bizarre scene unfolding, I couldn't help but think about the warnings my parents had given me about the bad behavior of people who frequented barrooms, and how I was headed for a life of ruin if I continued hanging around those dens of iniquity. I also couldn't help feeling a deep sense of sadness and embarrassment for this poor lady. This was somebody's grandmother making a pitiful fool of herself. Where was her family, and why weren't they taking better care of this lonely little soul?

> *For those who have worked the honky-tonks, the real Wild West show is not on the stage but more often provided by the audience. From my vantage point onstage, I have literally seen every part of the male and female anatomy: the good, the bad, and the ugly.*

For those who have worked the honky-tonks, the real Wild West show is not on the stage but more often provided by the audience. From my vantage point onstage, I have literally seen every part of the male and female anatomy: the good, the bad, and the ugly.

There are some sights you simply can't unsee.

THAT'S ANOTHER NOT-SO-FUNNY STORY

Over my fifty-plus years as a performing musician, I have witnessed, up close and personal, the devastating effects that addiction has had on too many of my talented friends. Be it whiskey, coke, crank, weed, opioids, prescription meds, gambling, cigarettes, sex, food, or any sort of obsessive- compulsive behavior, the results are always the same: Lives are cut short, careers are ruined or stunted, and families are devastated. I've seen gifted but troubled souls self-destruct right before my eyes.

Many of us spent a considerable amount of our careers playing music in seedy honky-tonks, bars, and dives. From our vantagepoint onstage, we saw people at their best: having fun, dancing, singing, laughing, falling in love, and celebrating life. We also saw them at their worst: fighting, staggering, puking, crying, cheating, falling out of love, and spiraling down into a drunken abyss from which many would never return. As musicians, we also experienced a lifestyle totally out-of-sync with the rest of the world. We worked until the wee hours of the morning, ate breakfast at three a.m., slept till noon, ate breakfast again at two in the afternoon, and socialized mostly with other musicians, waitresses, and other night owls. Being a nightclub entertainer is one of the few jobs where you are allowed, even encouraged, to drink on the job. Some drunk is always buying the band a round of tequila shots, some hanger-on is always there with a joint or a line, and fans of all stripes are always ready to party with the band. Over time, I discovered why my parents were so against me choosing a career that would place me in the proximity and with the occasion to partake of less-than-righteous behavior. I must admit I indulged in more than my share of debauchery, and it's only by the grace of God I was spared a ruinous life. I suppose that's the reason it became more and more troubling, despite my best attempts to help, to witness friends unable to control their appetites, never know when enough was enough, unable to stop their slide into oblivion, choosing their addictions over everything else in their lives.

One of the hardest things I ever had to do was cut my best friend out of my life. His alcoholism and drug abuse was one of the main causes of the breakup of our band, and his reluctance to accept my aid caused me tremendous heartache.

As the folks in Al-Anon say, you have to learn to accept the three C's when it comes to dealing with others' self-destructive behavior: I didn't Cause it; I can't Control it; I can't Cure it. Though these words have brought a blessed peace and serenity to my soul, it doesn't soften the sorrrow I feel that—for so many—death was perhaps the only relief their tortured souls could find.

THAT'LL BE A HUNDRED AND FIFTY EXPOSURES, PLEASE

I had a pick-up job one weekend playing guitar with my friend Dwaine Thomas' band at a little dive in Odessa, Texas. During one of the breaks, a drunk staggered over to the band table and said, "You guys is purty good; you oughta come on over t' Wink, Texas and play for us. We're hav'n a big ol' Roy Orbison Festival and you guys 'ud be great. It don't pay nutin' but you git lotsa exposure.

Jay Weatherby, the piano player, just looked at the guy and said, "You know, I'm a big ol' boy, and I like to eat a lot. The other day I was in the grocery store, and I loaded my cart up with some steaks, potatoes, onions, BBQ sauce, and all kinds of stuff. When I got to the checkout counter the cashier totaled up my groceries and said 'That'll be a hundred and fifty exposures, please.'"

Over the years, I've experienced that playing gigs for free to get "exposure" most often leads to being asked to play more gigs for more "exposure." Someone once remarked, "Don't you get arrested or die from exposure?"

part three

HEY, BO DIDDLEY

*"Baby, don't let yo' mouth
write a check yo' ass can't cash."*

- Bo Diddley

JUST DON'T STEP ON MY VOCALS

In September 1980 I had the magnificent honor to play with Bo Diddley at the Buddy Holly Memorial Festival in Lubbock, Texas. The event lineup included Bo Diddley, The Crickets with Sonny Curtis and guest, Waylon Jennings; and headliner, Roy Orbison. My friend, Suzanne Paulk (Henley), was in charge of putting together a band for Bo, as he generally traveled solo. Suzanne hired Royce Glen on drums, Chris Wilkerson on bass, Bonnie Wilkerson on keyboard, and me on guitar. I was honored, excited, and completely intimidated. This was, after all, The Bo Diddley!

We had been given a tentative song list, and were set up and ready for our two o'clock sound check, hoping to squeeze in a rehearsal run-through in the forty-five-minute window we were given. Bo and his road manager showed up about 3:30 p.m., and as we hurriedly tuned-up to run at least a couple of songs, Bo noticed two young gentlemen rolling a four-track recording machine past the stage toward the sound booth. He immediately put his guitar down, looked at his road manager, and yelled most emphatically, Oh hell no! He proceeded to launch into a tirade of all the times he had been ripped off by pirated recordings, and how he'd spent a frustrating part of his career trying to hunt down and stop all the people trying to steal his music and his money. "I ain't playin' this gig till they put that recorder back in the truck." Poor Suzanne was freaking out, and finally had to call the Mayor of Lubbock and the concert promoters to come convince Bo that nobody was trying to cheat him.

As it turns out, Paul McCartney had actually wanted to come to the show, but had scheduling conflicts, so his people had contacted Don Caldwell studios to request that Don make a live recording of the show to send to Paul for his private listening pleasure. Bo was finally convinced that the recording would not be marketed, and though our rehearsal

Bo Diddley, Cary Banks, Royce Glen Live performance Lubbock Civic Center, September 1980 Photo courtesy - A Summer Moon video archive/ Greg Cook

time was pretty much gone, we did manage to get a brief run-through of Bo's signature song, Bo Diddley. Royce, the drummer, had been practicing for days, trying to perfect the tom tom drum part on the song, but only about eight bars into the tune Bo stopped and said "Hey, drummer man, I don't use that drum beat no mo'; just stay on your hi hat." He then looked at me through those big, square coke-bottle-bottom glasses, and said, "Play what you want to, gittar man; just don't step on my vocals."

Just as we were about to take the stage, Bo refused to go on until he got his money. Radio personality, Jerry Bo Coleman, had been assigned the duty of hanging with Bo all day to make sure everything was taken care of, and this was yet another glitch in an already-stressful day. Radio station owner, Larry Corbin, who had booked Bo for the show, was told Bo would not go on stage until he had the money in his hand. Once again, Suzanne had to step up. She went to the box office, got the cash, and promptly delivered it to Bo. I seem to remember that Bo's manager took it and locked it in Bo's guitar case, and I don't think the case ever left the manager's grasp.

As we took our places on the stage, the audience began to chant, Bo! Bo! Bo! The chant grew louder as he sauntered to the center of the stage, plugged that trademark cigar-box-shaped guitar into his amp, turned it up all the way, strummed a big fat open E chord, and launched into the signature guitar riff of Bo Diddley. The audience went absolutely crazy, and Bo delivered an unforgettable, soulful, and masterful performance as only he could do, sometimes interjecting talkin' blues lines such as: "Baby, don't let yo' mouth write a check yo' ass can't cash."

I don't remember a lot of what I played that night, although through the miracle of the internet I discovered a Youtube video of that concert showing me playing a decent solo on the song You Can't Judge a Book by It's Cover. Mostly what I remember is that for forty-five minutes I was in musical heaven playing guitar on stage with . . . Bo Diddley.

WEST TEXAS OPRY

One of the most exciting, fun, and musically rewarding shows I had the pleasure of performing on was the West Texas Opry. The Opry was produced by Don Caldwell and directed by the incomparable Lloyd Maines. While we may have "borrowed" the Opry name from the Grand Ol' Opry in Nashville, we certainly gave the show our own brand of pickin' and grinin', and under the guidance of Lloyd Maines, produced a professional-quality show that would compare with any big-time production, anywhere, anytime. I played guitar in the Opry stage band, which was

Rockin' the country music show Cary Banks, Steve Maines, Donnie Maines Lloyd Maines and Kenny Maines
Photo courtesy - Robert Hudnal

basically The Maines Brothers Band and a few other select West Texas musicians. The featured performers included gospel artists, western swing artists, country singers, and pickers and songwriters from all around the West Texas area. Many of the performers such as Terri Sue Caldwell, David House, The Angle Sisters, and Jim Fulingim were well- known in the West Texas area, and had recorded highly successful albums and singles at Caldwell Recording studio. The Opry that I was involved with ran from 1977 to 1983, and played to packed concert halls about four times a year. The show was sponsored by local radio station KLLL 96.3 FM, and was, in my opinion, one of the most successful locally-produced music events in West Texas history. The Opry was even featured in the December 23, 1978 issue of Billboard magazine. Many West Texas music fans fondly recall the highly entertaining, exciting, and professional productions of the West Texas Opry, with such memorable moments as Johnny Ray Watson's big, booming baritone belting out Ol' Man River, or Cecil Caldwell and his famous Tap Dancin' Board. Or the time trumpeter Tommy Anderson brought the Monterey High School Marching Band, in full marching uniforms, onstage to jam with the Opry Band. All of us involved with the Opry productions knew, from the very first shows, that we were part of something very special. The West Texas Opry inspired countless young musicians and influenced a host of other country and gospel music shows that came along later.

. . . AND THEN THE MIDGET SANG

I am honored to have played on a few of singer/songwriter/visual artist, Terry's Allen's, recordings: Bloodlines, Smokin', The Dummy, Rollback, and the soundtrack to the film, Amerasia.* I also had the musically magical experience of playing several live gigs with Terry as a member of the notorious Panhandle Mystery Band. To say the least, all the gigs were eventful, but one that stands out is the time we played at an art gallery in Santa Fe, New Mexico.

The entire weekend was an event, including a huge barbeque dinner catered by C. B. Stubbefield, aka "Stubbs." As usual, Terry was accompa-

Back stage at a Terry Allen Santa Fe show: Richard Bowden, Joe Ely, Donnie Maines, Terry Allen, Cary Banks, Kenny Maines, Lloyd Maines, C B "Stubbs" Stubbefield
Photo courtesy - Cary Banks Collection

nied by an eclectic entourage of artists, musicians, hippies, philosophers, etc. Among the noteworthy was performer and songwriter, Joe Ely, and his entourage, which included Stubbs and faithful companion, Little Pete. The show was held in the big room of the gallery, which accommodated around two hundred people. The room had a nice, spacious stage about three feet above the gallery floor.

The Panhandle Mystery Band gigs were designed to be an event, featuring Terry's art and a live performance by the band. Terry's music is a unique, eclectic mix of country, folk, blues, rock, and Americana, with lyrics picturing an unholy host of disparate characters: Carnival barkin' preachers, sullen artists, fallen saints, fallen football legends, truck drivin' wild men, and rollin' pen-wieldin' heart-of-gold women. The music is driven by Terry's thumpin', bumpin', poundin' piano playing, and his rough and ragged, half singin', half shoutin', in yer face vocals. The musical dynamics of his shows usually started at double forte and got increasing louder, more driving, and more intense.

This particular incarnation of the Mystery Band featured Terry on piano and lead vocal, Donnie Maines on drums, Kenny Maines on bass, Lloyd Maines, (the leader of the group) on acoustic, electric, and pedal steel guitar, Richard Bowden on fiddle and mandolin, and me playing electric guitar. Toward the end of the show, Joe Ely jumped on stage and started singing with Terry. As we launched into a manic, punk rock version of Buddy Holly's Not Fade Away, Joe began pulling people from the floor onto the stage. By the end of the song, everybody in the art gallery was onstage, including Stubbs and Little Pete. Pete stood about three feet nothin' and was quite a performer in his own right, famous for his blues vocals and his impersonations of celebrities, including Alfred Hitchcock. The song was a colossal mix of ear-bleeding, open-ringing E guitar chords, slashing cymbals, pounding, heart-stopping bass and drums, and a chorus of two hundred voices screaming NOT FADE AWAY, NOT FADE AWAY, NOT FADE AWAY.

As the song ended, I saw people stepping all over my guitar cables and effects pedal, and Terry's two young sons, Bukka and Bale, riding my Yamaha amplifier (with wheels) like a rocking horse down the back of the stage toward the loadout door. An article about the show appeared in the Santa Fe newspaper art section featuring the famous headline "... and then the midget sang."

A photo of Terry, Joe Ely, Stubbs, Richard Bowden; Kenny, Donnie, and Lloyd Maines and me backstage was included in the Joe Carr and Alan Munde award-winning book about West Texas music and musicians, "Prairie Nights, To Neon Lights."

The performances were always magical, mystical, rowdy, inspiring, and exhilarating ... and something of mine almost always got broken.

Performing onstage with either Terry Allen or Joe Ely was always a glorious adventure and a mixed blessing for me. The performances were always magical, mystical, rowdy, inspiring, and exhilarating ... and something of mine almost always got broken.

MR. SOUL AND THE INFAMOUS COTTON CLUB INCIDENT

In the spring of 1982 a group of creative high school students got together and decided they wanted to throw their own Prom Night. About a hundred or so friends pooled their money, convinced a handful of parents to chaperone, rented the infamous Cotton Club, east of Lubbock, and hired the Maines Brothers Band to provide entertainment for this festive evening. The prom event just happened to be scheduled on the eve of Joe Ely's Third Annual Tornado Jam, which would commence the following day at Buddy Holly Park. It had been a particularly wet spring, and this May evening was no exception. The back of the club, where we were to load-in our equipment, was flooded; the bathrooms were flooded; and the parking lot was mostly flooded. None of that seemed to faze the eager, young partygoers, who showed up dressed in their big prom dresses and rented tuxedos, ready to party. We had developed a loyal following among high school students by playing school assemblies and throwing an annual Panhandle Dance exclusively for them.

The kids were dancing and having a blast. There was no trouble—even the parents seemed to be having a good time. We were scheduled to play till midnight; and sometime after 11:00 p.m., the front doors swung open, and in walked Joe Ely, arm-in-arm with Linda Ronstadt, and followed by Little Feat's keyboardist, Billy Payne; Jesse Taylor, Terry Allen, Butch Hancock, Jimmie Dale Gilmore, Ponty Bone, and a holy host of other musicians. The stunned dancers stood there, mouths gaping, thinking: Holy Crap! Is that Linda Ronstadt? All the Ely entourage squeezed onto the stage; someone played a big E Chord, Linda belted out, "WELLLLLLL . . . That'll be the day . . . " The entire place erupted in screams, cheers, and pandemonium. Linda's voice was so rich and powerful she might not have even needed a PA, but with this gaggle of musicians—I counted eighteen people on the stage, all with noise makers in their hands—it was one giant wall of eardrum-splitting sound blasting from the stage.

> *The entire place erupted in screams, cheers, and pandemonium.*

Linda Ronstadt, Joe Ely, The Maines Brothers Band and A Holy Host of others, on stage at The Cotton Club, Lubbock, Texas
Photo courtesy: Milton Adams

A photo of this event hung in a popular local restaurant for years. However, there is no trace of me in the picture because I was playing guitar and standing behind someone ferociously whacking away on a cowbell. The only way I could keep from getting smacked in the face with his drumstick was to crouch down behind him and somehow keep playing while perched on one knee. Joe and Linda traded country tunes, blues, and swing, and the whole thing was a monumental musical event that would have probably gone on until the wee hours, but the flunky in charge of the venue barged up to the stage at midnight and declared the party over. Of course that met with a collective audience scream of "NOOOOOOOOO. We want more music." That did not deter the flunky—who Terry Allen later dubbed "Mr. Soul—from walking to the back of the club and turning off all the power switches. I think someone even offered to pay him extra to let the party go a little longer, but he was having none of it. His shift was over, and it was time for everyone to leave. After a loud and sustained chorus of boos and This sucks, man! the party goers reluctantly gave up and made their way out the door, still reeling from the event they had just witnessed.

I estimated there were probably around 150 to 200 young folks and parents in the Cotton Club that night. Over the years it seems there have been thousands of people who claimed to have been there that evening ... but that's the stuff of legends and urban myths.

Photo courtesy - Maines Brothers Collection

part four

THE MAINES BROTHERS BAND

"The problem with surrendering your will and giving all your problems to God is, He acts like He has all the time in the world."

- Matt Smith

A HONKY TONK PIANO MAN IN A ROCKIN' LITTLE COUNTRY BAND

I met Lloyd Maines in 1974 at Don Caldwell studios in Lubbock, Texas. I had been living in Dallas for a couple of years and had returned to Lubbock and started, once again, working at Jent's House of Music. I had heard of Lloyd, whose impressive reputation preceded him everywhere he went. The first time I ever played a gig with him, all the hype about his phenomenal musicianship and steel guitar prowess was definitely confirmed. I had met several terrific musicians in my time, and he was at the top of the list. I played several gigs and worked a few recording sessions with him, and it was during one of the recording sessions that I first met Kenny Maines. When I heard him tracking vocals in the studio, it proved his reputation as one of the best singers in West Texas. Shortly after I returned to Lubbock, I also met a very young Donnie Maines who was already an excellent drummer. I met Steve Maines when I became a part of the West Texas Opry band, and it was during its many successful shows that I developed what would become a lifelong friendship with the members of this elite family of West Texas musicians. At the time, Randy Brownlow was playing piano in the Maines Brothers band, and his brother, Jerry, was bass player and vocalist. Richard Bowden had just joined as fiddler, and I had the wonderful opportunity to sit in with the group on numerous occasions. One of the most noteworthy was when we opened a show for the rising country superstar group, Alabama.

Guitar had always been my principal instrument, but since the day my Aunt Myrtle gave me her old upright piano, I had been fascinated with the keyboard. I taught myself to play it much as I had taught myself the guitar, by watching other players, listening to thousands of hours of recordings and radio, and sitting down at any piano I ever stumbled

Playing piano with my feet like Jerry Lee
Photo courtesy: T G Caraway Collection/Southwest Collection/Special Collections Library/ Texas Tech University, Lubbock, Texas

---

across. Whenever I was invited to a home that had a piano, most of the time I didn't even ask; I just sat down and started playing. By the late 1970's and early 80's, I had become a pretty good, well-rounded guitar player who also played a little piano.

In early 1983, the Maines Brothers band, having just released their Panhandle Dancer album, were starting to get interest from record labels in Nashville and were ready to embark on an extensive touring schedule. At that point, deciding to focus his energies on his secure job in the oil field, Randy Brownlow resigned his position as the band's pianist.

One evening out of the blue, I received a call from Lloyd Maines, who told me about Randy leaving the band, and said that he and the other members had agreed to offer me the job. To say the least, I was stunned. I had worked with them many times, but mostly as a guitarist. In addition, there were several keyboard players in the area who were, in all honesty, better than me. Nevertheless, they offered me the opportunity to not only join the band, but to become a permanent member of the Maines Brothers business partnership. I accepted the position with much gratitude—and I must admit—a certain trepidation. I was primarily a guitarist, but from that moment on, I was a full-time piano player. I had begun my musical journey on the guitar and had always thought, visually and technically, in terms of that instrument, attempting to translate what I knew on it to the piano. I had honed my guitar skills trying to copy guitar masters like Chet Atkins, Andres Segovia, the Beatles, the Rolling Stones, country guitarists like Don Rich, jazz artists like Wes Montgomery, and songwriters like Mickie Newbury and Paul Simon. However, taking on the piano as my primary instrument was a bit like learning to speak a second language. Now all of a sudden I had to learn to think in piano. It was a hard struggle and it took me a couple of years before I really became confident with it. I had fashioned my limited keyboard skills trying to learn to play like my songwriting heroes: Jimmy Webb, Randy Newman, Carole King, and others. I had always been intrigued by the charismatic and blues-influenced black and southern gospel piano players, and the energetic and groovy piano stylings of New Orleans keyboardists like Dr. John and Huey "Piano" Smith. Later on, I really came to admire the skills and creativity of Nashville session players such as Floyd Cramer and Hargus "Pig" Robbins, and California "Wrecking Crew" players like Leon Russell and Larry Knetchtel. I also learned so much from my friend, Jewette James, a phenomenal western swing pianist who had worked with John Lee Wills and many others in that genre back in the 50's and '60's. I was also fortunate to go to high school with, and learn, by osmosis, from one of the greatest piano players I've ever known: David Crawford.

Someone once asked me if it was hard switching from guitar to piano. I seem to remember thinking, "I guess it's no harder than switching from trombone to violin." That bit of sarcasm aside, I must admit that one of the downsides of my new career instrument was that as I got better on the piano, my guitar skills began to atrophy. I tried to keep up a practice schedule on guitar as well, but woodshedding on piano and songwriting, while trying to be a good husband and father to two small children, didn't leave much margin to spend time with my first musical love.

I don't regret my decision in the least. I still love to play the guitar, and I became a pretty decent Honky Tonk Piano Man in a Rockin' Little Country Band.

WHEN 'ER YOU GUYS GONNA GO PERFESHNUL?

By the spring of 1983, The Maines Brothers Band had already produced four albums on Texas Soul Records and opened shows for some of the biggest acts in country music, including Alabama, Ronnie Millsap, Dr Hook, and countless others. The band was an official Limited Liability Partnership, with a huge regional following. We had recorded music for Stella Steven's independent film, "American Woman," played some of the most famous honky-tonks in the country, including Billy Bob's Texas, Gilleys, and the Lone Star Café in New York City, and had signed a recording contract with Mercury Records Nashville.

Steve Maines and me taping the Austin City Limits TV show.
Photo courtesy - Austin City Limits TV show video/Greg Cook

One evening Steve Maines was at the grocery store in Lubbock when the young man carrying his groceries to the car bluntly posed a question. "When 'er you guys gonna go perfeshnul?" A quintessential West Texas cowboy teenager, he was a fan of country music in general and The Maines Brothers Band in specific.

This type of question had been asked of Steve before, and good natured as he is, he always tried to find a non-condescending, humorous way to answer. He replied, "Well, we've run the numbers, and there's just not enough profit in it for us." As usual, his answer was met with a blank expression and a mystified, "Huh?"

Over the years, I've heard several people express the thought that a lot of folks expected The Maines Brothers Band to become the next Beatles, and were surprised when we didn't catch on to a world-wide audience. Others have said that we were just years ahead of our time.

I guess the young man at the grocery store assumed the band was "Almost like Professional."

COLD WATER COUNTRY

For decades, West Texas has been home to some of the most unique, colorful, and story-filled country music dance halls in the nation. The legendary Stampede in Big Spring, Texas has been owned and operated by the Nix family since the early 1950's, and today is still home of the Texas Cowboys, led by Jody Nix. There have been many other well-known establishments around the West Texas area, including The Palm Room, The Saddle Bronc, and The Cow Palace, but the one country dance club that stands out , especially during the 70's and early '80's, was the infamous Cold Water Country. The spacious building, constructed in the late 50's or early 60's at the corner of University Avenue and what would later become South Loop 289, was originally a bowling alley, and a few years later, a furniture store. When the store went out of business, the building was converted to a country music dance hall named The Hall of Fame, where the original Maines Brothers Band (James Maines and his brothers) and the "Little Maines Brothers" (Kenny , Lloyd and

Maines Brothers Band on stage at the infamous Coldwater Country Nightclub and dance hall
Photo courtesy - TG Caraway Collection/ Southwest Collection/Special Collections Library/Texas Tech University, Lubbock, Texas

Steve) performed. A few years later, the club changed ownership and was renamed the Bigger'N Dallas nightclub.

My first foray into this historic nightspot in the mid 70's was to see rising Texas music stars Asleep at the Wheel. The opening act that evening, the regular house band, was popular local artist, Bobby Albright and his band, Boot hill Express. I had no way of knowing that the bass player for Boot Hill Express, Jerry Brownlow, would later become my band mate in The Maines Brothers Band, and one of my closest personal friends. During Bobby Albright's time as house band at Bigger'N Dallas, his friend and club owner, James Witt, was shot to death in the parking lot outside the club by a disgruntled employee. Not long after that incident, Bobby packed up his band and moved to Anchorage, Alaska, where he would become a headline performer for years. I had the opportunity to play a country and swing gig at Bigger'N Dallas with my friend, Johnny James, his dad, fiddler Buzz James, and his mom, swing piano player, Jewette James.

When Bigger'N Dallas closed its doors, the building was purchased by some investors intent on remodeling the establishment and reopening it as a major country western dance club called Coldwater Cattle Company. The name was changed to simply, Cold Water Country. I was working at the time at Jack T's Music World, owned by my friend, Jack Tyson. Jack was friends with the gentleman who had contracted to install a new sound and lighting system for the revamped nightclub. Jack had made a deal with the contractor to outfit the new club with a massive state-of-the-art Cerwin Vega sound system. Part of the deal was that Jack had agreed to fly to Los Angeles, where the Cerwin Vega plant was located, rent a large Ryder truck, and transport the mammoth system back to Lubbock for installation. The window of time available for retrieving it, bringing it back, and having it installed was very narrow, so Jack asked me to accompany him on this little adventure. We flew out from Lubbock on a Friday afternoon, packed the truck early that Saturday morning, and left Los Angeles, taking turns driving until we arrived back in Lubbock with our cargo that following Monday evening.

Shortly afterward, the club had its grand opening with a special appearance by country music legend, Merle Haggard. The show was a phenomenal success, and for the next seven years, Cold Water Country would host some of country music's biggest stars, including Asleep at the Wheel, Ray Price, Mickey Gilley, Gary Stewart, Rusty Weir, Joe Ely, and countless others. The club also featured local bands performing Tuesday through Saturday, and was famous for its "Crash and Burn" Wednesday Nights, featuring free drinks for the ladies and half-price, long neck beer. That particular event was especially attractive for college students from Texas Tech. (The drinking age was eighteen back then.)

Some of my personal favorite memories of performing at Cold Water Country include Halloween night in 1978, when the Free Whiskey Band played country music dressed in full makeup as the group Kiss. We called ourselves KUSS. Another memorable evening happened when the Joe Ely Band took the stage. Joe rode in through the front door, all the way through the packed dance floor to the front of the stage . . . on a horse.

One evening, I was blessed with an opportunity to be backstage with country star Razzy Bailey and pitched him some of my original songs.

The club served as a gathering place for thousands of music fans, dancers, lovers, dreamers, and famous, infamous, and hoping-to-be-discovered musicians. It was not uncommon, especially when Joe Ely was performing, for the crowd to greatly exceed the 2,000 maximum occupancy allowed by the fire marshal. Thursday mornings, following the infamous "Crash and Burn" Wednesday nights, would find the floor of the club knee-deep in Lone Star beer and MD2020 wine bottles.

The front lounge also served as a meeting place for the West Texas Music Association board meetings, and a secret hideout from out-of-control fans, crazy ex-girlfriends, and mannerless drunks. It was also a place where we gathered after hours to hear Gordie Hamm, aka Ramblin' Rose, regale us with wild stories and jokes. One of the fondest memories several of us in The Maines Brothers Band share is that at the close of every night, the last song sound man and DJ, Joe Piland, played over the sound system was Merle Haggard's beautiful and plaintive ballad, Here in Frisco. Of course, that tender moment was often destroyed by Gordie Hamm, who—if customers were still hanging around after closing time—would empty the building by turning up the volume on the sound system as loud as it would go, and playing a marching-band rendition of the The Star-Spangled Banner. Usually, by the end of the song, only cockroaches and deaf bartenders were left in the building.

> *Usually, by the end of the song, only cockroaches and deaf bartenders were left in the building.*

I've been fortunate to perform in some of the most famous honkytonk dance halls in the world, including Billy Bob's Texas, The Palomino Club in LA, and several others. That being said, the old adage, "A bar is a bar is a bar" has proven true to me over and over. I spent many an evening on that Cold Water Country stage with the Free Whiskey Band, Joey Allen and Almost Live with the Celestial sisters, Gwen Decker, Suzanne Henley and Bonnie Mcrae, the Mike Porter Band, The Maines Brothers Band, Terry Allen and the Panhandle Mystery Band, and others. I had so many wonderful musical memories there, but in truth, it was a bar like any other. The lights on stage were unbearably hot, the whole place reeked of stale beer, cigarettes, and puke, and more than a few drummers fell backwards off the stage as there was no wall or railing there. One night, a blind singer almost took a head-dive off the front of the stage.

Despite the not-so-exotic underbelly of the club, in its heyday Cold Water Country was a hotspot of high- energy country and country rock that transformed a budding generation of young up-and-coming West Texas musicians. Sadly, New Year's Eve 1984 was the final performance of The Maines Brothers Band at Cold Water Country, as the club closed its doors the next day.

After its closing, the club reopened a couple of years later as Murphy's, and later changed its name to Midnight Rodeo. It eventually closed its doors a final time in the late 90's, and the building and all surrounding property was razed and replaced by a strip mall.

There is a generation of musicians and music lovers for which the Cold Water Country nightclub in Lubbock, Texas will always hold a special place. In our many travels across the country, from California to New York, invariably someone would come up to us after a show to say they had gone to school at Texas Tech, and to tell us how much fun they had dancing to The Maines Brothers Band at Cold Water Country.

THE RECORD DEAL

Almost without exception every garage band, local talent-show singer, or American Idol Wanna Be clings to the same shiny, glitter-filled dream of signing the sacred music business document, the Record Deal. That multi-page document that only the most educated and devious legal minds can decipher. The one that says some music business hotshot movers-and-shakers believe you are indeed the next Elvis, or Beatles, or Lady Gaga, and that makes grandiose promises to sink millions of dollars into your recordings, promotion, and publicity, and make you a STAR. The sad reality is the music business highway is littered with

The Maines Brothers Band with business manager, Paul Godwin, signing our recording contract with Mercury Records
Photo courtesy - Maines Brothers Collection

the remains of talented people who essentially signed away their lives, their dreams, their fortunes, and souls, all on the thin, ethereal hope and promise of becoming a star. Despite all the cautionary tales told by the countless victims of this eternal pipe dream, every new generation puts its hopes and dreams in that one shiny, glitter-filled basket.

By the time I joined The Maines Brothers Band, I had been in the music business long enough and had experienced enough shattered hopes and expectations that I wasn't as impressed with the thought of signing a major label record deal as in my younger days. I'd seen plenty of promises and sure-deals fall flat, so I was leery when Lloyd Maines traveled to Nashville to meet with executives of Mercury/Polygram Records to discuss the possibility of the band signing a record deal. Lloyd had previously dealt with a major label, MCA, when he was part of the Joe Ely Band, so this was definitely not his first rodeo. Several major labels had expressed interest in the band, and Mercury Records had actually sent one of its staff, Rick Peoples, to Lubbock to hear us perform live. The Maines Brothers Band had already produced four record albums on the independent label, Texas Soul Records, and had developed quite a large regional fan base; and the bigwigs at Mercury could see the group was an established, successful enterprise. We discovered later that the record company executives had originally wanted to sign only the four brothers, Lloyd, Steve, Kenny, and Donnie. Lloyd was quite adamant that the band was comprised of seven members and any deal would include all of them. Not only that, Lloyd insisted that all recordings be done at Don Caldwell studios in Lubbock, with all the tracks recorded using band members, not Nashville studio players. I must say that was a pretty bold move on his part, but he knew the vision of the band and what we wanted to accomplish, and as I said, this wasn't his first rodeo. The folks at Mercury agreed to Lloyd's proposals, and preparations for contracts, studio time, and promotion began.

Lloyd was excited when he returned to Lubbock and presented the news to the rest of us. The funniest part was him sharing that—right in the middle of serious negotiations—one of the record company execs had fallen sound asleep in his chair.

Local newsprint media made a big deal of our record deal, featuring a picture of the band with our business manager, Paul Godwin, signing the big record contract. Lloyd caused a bit of a stir when he was quoted in the newspaper saying the band was excited and ready to go out in the world and "kick ass." There was some good-natured chastisement from moms and grand-moms about Lloyd's language, but a more controversial moment came when he made an off-hand comment that we wouldn't be recording any songs about "tight-fittin' jeans," the theme of a recent hit country song that we considered cheesy and lame. Some of the folks at Mercury weren't happy that Lloyd had publicly dissed a hit song. I guess they didn't understand that out in West Texas we tend to speak our minds, regardless of what the rest of the world might think. Anyway, they got over it and we forged on.

The contract was twenty-five pages long and filled with all kinds of legalese and music business mumbo jumbo: Party of the first part and Forthwith in perpetuity recoupable stuff. We all read it, re-read it, had our business manager, Paul Godwin, read it; Paul hired Charlie Pride's attorney to read it; and we came to the conclusion that it was a pretty standard record deal contract, with the record company in control of most of the options. Nevertheless, we affixed our names to the document and agreed to a multi-year, multi-album record deal with Mercury/Polygram Recording Company.

In spite of my somewhat jaded past music business disappointments, I found myself almost giddy at the thought of signing a real-life, honest-to-goodness major label record contract. I remember being at home later that day after our signing soiree, staring out my kitchen window thinking, "Man, I'm with a band that just signed a major record deal. How absolutely cool am I?" Of course, I was immediately brought back to reality when I realized at that exact moment that I was right in the middle of washing a sink full of dirty dishes. That moment would prove to be a harbinger of things to come.

We began working on our first album, High Rollin,' with legendary producer, Jerry Kennedy, at Don Caldwell studios in Lubbock. Mr. Kennedy, Nashville recording engineer Lou Bradley, and Mercury Records A&R Man, Rick Peoples, flew to Lubbock from Nashville to record and produce the album.

> *"Man, I'm with a band that just signed a major record deal. How absolutely cool am I?" Of course, I was immediately brought back to reality when I realized at that exact moment that I was right in the middle of washing a sink full of dirty dishes.*

We had some memorable moments during that first session. We began recording the album in the heat of the summer, and right in the middle of the session the air conditioning unit broke down. We didn't have the luxury of waiting for it to be repaired, so we recorded several tracks late at night, wearing a minimum of clothing. Fortunately, I don't think any photos of those sessions survived.

During those first sessions, we were also the beneficiaries of a full blown, no-holds-barred, good old-fashioned home-cooked buffet dinner, whipped up by the brother's grandmother, MaMaw Maines. The giant spread included the traditional West Texas fare of fried chicken, meatloaf, green bean casserole, mashed potatoes, carrots, okra, homemade biscuits, and everybody's favorite "nanner pudding" (banana pudding for those not raised in the South). It truly was a feast fit for kings, served with the love and pride only a grandmother can provide. Looking back, it might not have been the best idea to serve that meal at lunch, as by the time we had all gorged ourselves silly, none of us were really up for recording any high-energy Aggressive Country Music tracks. At one point during that afternoon session, we noticed that our legendary producer, Jerry Kennedy, had fallen victim to the aftereffects of MaMaw Maines' bountiful buffet, and was "resting his eyes" briefly during one of the takes.

We were so fortunate to work with such a legendary producer. Jerry had played guitar for country superstar, Johnny Horton, had played the soulful and oh-so-catchy dobro part on Jeannie C. Riley's smash hit, Harper Valley PTA, had played guitar on Roy Orbison's Pretty Woman, and had produced such well-known artists as Roger Miller, Tom T. Hall, Jerry Lee Lewis, and the Statler Brothers. He is a gracious, intelligent, and humble man who was easy to work with, and gave us enormous creative freedom in the studio. He's also very funny and kept us thoroughly entertained with a multitude of stories, especially those of producing the Statler Brother's hilarious album, Lester Road Hog Moran and the Cadillac Cowboys, Saturday Mornin' Radio Show. I think he could quote every line from that uproariously funny record.

Our first Mercury album produced a couple of singles that made a modest showing on the charts, including You Are a Miracle that Jerry Brownlow and I had written. We signed with Barbara Mandrel's booking agency and were booked on a couple of national tours with her. We performed on some major TV shows, including Austin City Limits and TNN's Nashville Now, got our picture in People Magazine, and purchased a Silver Eagle tour bus. It appeared we were on our way to some major success in the entertainment industry. (*More bus details later*)

Mercury records was sufficiently pleased with our performance and asked for a second album, which produced the single, Everybody Needs Love on a Saturday Night, that made it to Number 21 on the Billboard Country Charts. We were fortunate to work with ace engineer, Brent King, on our second album, and it appeared we were on our way once again.

We did make some wonderful friends and valuable connections, but chasing radio, as most artists will attest, is like chasing the wind. As soon as you think you've caught it, it's gone without a trace.

An interesting phenomena in the music industry is that a hit record can be both a blessing and a curse. When a record company releases a single for one of its artists, the process of "chasing radio" begins. The record company employs both staff and independent record promoters to call, wine and dine, connive, cajole, and otherwise convince radio stations to add a new song to their playlists. Hopefully, the listening public will like the song, call in to the station frequently to request it, and hopefully purchase the single and/or the album. The artist is equally tasked with promotion of the record, so we relentlessly called radio stations, visited them for interviews and live on-air performances, played impromptu softball games with the staff, and gave them free passes to our shows and access to backstage where they helped themselves to our drinks and food—all for the purpose of creating friendly relationships with the DJ's, owners, managers, and staff. We did make some wonderful friends and valuable connections, but chasing radio, as most artists will attest, is like chasing the wind. As soon as you think you've caught it, it's gone without a trace.

With our initial success came the realization we would be traveling more and farther to promote ourselves nationwide, and that necessitated a more accommodating travel vehicle than our beloved, but way past its prime, motor home. We purchased our tour bus from Jay Boy Adams Roadhouse Bus Company soon after signing our recording contract. One of the most beautiful and unique Silver Eagles on the road, with its exotic murals of '57 Chevys painted on the sides, it caught the attention of many motorists and fans as we scorched the asphalt from one end of the country to the other, touring with Barbara Mandrel and other acts.

However, between the monthly payments, expensive insurance, gas-guzzling fuel costs, driver salaries, and constant maintenance bills, that giant piece of rolling real estate was one mammoth mobile money pit. I can honestly say that one of the happiest days of my life was when, thanks to the tireless efforts of Lloyd Maines, we finally sold it to a gospel group in California. Praise the Lord . . . and Praise the Lloyd.

After the modest success of Everybody Needs Love on a Saturday Night, the record company released a couple more singles but they received little, if any, attention. We began to feel as if we might not be a top priority act at Mercury Records. We were burning up the highway playing shows from Utah to New York but it seemed our progress was, as Bruce Springsteen sang, One step up and two steps back. As we began cutting tracks for what would be our third album for Mercury, Lloyd had a meeting with some record company executives to figure how best to move the band forward. We found out sometime later that the record promoters were told by many radio stations that The Maines Brothers Band was just "too rock for country and too country for rock." The final blow may have been when Lloyd tried to convince the record execs to produce a music video to promote us. This was in 1987, and MTV was the hottest thing in all media; TNN was beginning to air country music videos; and new networks like Country Music Television (CMT) and Great American Country (GAC) were on the horizon. Lloyd was told that the company felt that music videos were not that essential in promoting country music at that time, and that the extra expense of producing one was not something they could give the green light. At this point, some of our closest allies at the label had moved on to other pursuits, and it appeared to us we were not at the top of the radar screen at Mercury Records.

When Lloyd brought us back the news, it was pretty obvious that we could all see the inevitable. After some cussing and discussing, we agreed to ask Mercury to release us from our contract. That was a brave and bold move on our part, as record companies generally decide when and if they will release an artist. The folks at Mercury were actually quite gracious, and we quietly and uneventfully parted company.

For me personally, losing the record contract with Mercury was a sad resignation to the inevitable, but even more, a sense of something left unfinished. It also meant I now had even less of a chance of getting a major label cut on any of my songs. We had started with such confidence, promise, and potential and were left with the frustrating realization that so much of our career was completely out of our control.

After we severed our ties with Mercury Records, we recorded two more albums, Red Hot and Blue, and Windstorm, on our independent record label, Texas Soul. We recorded my original instrumental song, Panhandle Serenade for the Red Hot And Blue album, and Let The Rain Come Down and Gonna Be a Cowboy for the Windstorm album. After Windstorm, the band slowed down our touring schedule considerably, and by the early 1990's, we had virtually stopped performing altogether. Though we remained friends, we inevitably all found new career opportunities. In August 2000, we had the glorious opportunity to reunite as a band and perform as the opening act for a little group from Texas known as the Dixie Chicks.

In truth, we made good music before we signed with Mercury Records, and we continued to make good music after we left.

THE LONELINESS OF THE HEARTBROKEN SONGWRITER

Anyone who has ever tried to write a song has probably experienced—in one degree or another—what a lonely endeavor it can become. Certainly, anyone who has ever longed to have their song published by a major publisher, recorded by a well-known artist or label, or played on their favorite radio station knows those desires can lead down that long hard road to heartbreak and despair. If you happen to have any success, you soon realize how lucky that success is, and how frustrating it is to spend the rest of your life trying to recapture it.

We songwriters write because we have something to say, and pouring out the feelings of our heart and soul with words and music is the best way we know how to do it. We all want the fame and money that comes with writing a hit song that sells millions of copies (or billions of downloads and streams), but more than anything else we want an audience, that incomparable bond between author and listener. The loneliness and heartbreak comes with the incredibly hard process of getting your song from that little scrap of paper to the lo-fi recording on your tape recorder or iPhone, then to its glorious master recording, and finally, past the gate keepers in the music business that combine to build a wall between you and your coveted million-fan audience.

Fifty years of fighting the good fight in the music business has taught me many lessons, especially in the songwriting realm. Among the harsh realities I've learned is that there are millions of people who fancy themselves songwriters, and sadly, most of them are not good, yet they seem to be the ones who think themselves great and are the most offended if you make the tiniest negative comment about their song.

The truth of the matter is that it's really hard to write a good, original song, and it's next-to-impossible to write a great one. However, even the most rank amateur never gives up the hope that one day that magic hit tune will miraculously fall in their lap.

I do understand how songwriters become emotionally attached to their songs. Superstar Lionel Richie said his songs are like children to him. When I first began trying to write, I soon discovered that there was much about the craft that I didn't know. I would listen to such incredibly great songs as Wichita Lineman or Hey Jude, or terrific hymns such as Great is Thy Faithfulness, and would think, "How in the world did they come up with that?" Or "How did they know to put that chord with that melody?" At that time there were virtually no schools, with the exception of Julliard School of Music, that even remotely dealt with the art and craft of popular songwriting. There were precious few books in print that discussed the subject, and definitely no internet, YouTube videos, or online songwriting classes. Other than Hoyle Nix and Ben Hall, I had never met any professional songwriters. It wasn't until 1979 that I ran across a cassette course on songwriting called The Complete Songwriter by the late Buddy Kaye. That little cassette changed my life. My only regret is that it wasn't recorded and published years earlier in my career.

Like all songwriters who have tried to make it in the business, my career has been a roller coaster ride full of a few exhilarating highs, but an insufferable number of heartbreaking lows, both for me and a few of my talented co-writers. The ride goes something like this:

THE SONGS: PART ONE

ALBUQUERQUE CALLIN' AND DON'T GET INVOLVED
VAN STANSELL AND ROBIN GRIFFIN

I met my friend, Van Stansell, a talented saxophonist and all-around musician, at Lubbock Christian College, and we hit it off musically right away. We wrote a couple of songs while in school, and later he and I became roommates. We decided we would be the next Lennon/McCartney songwriting duo and agreed to split, 50/50, every song we wrote separately or together. Bad idea. Though we did collaborate on a few songs, there were several tunes that I wrote completely by myself, including Albuquerque Callin' that still bore both our names on the credits. That would later lead to some hard feelings on my part and a vow to never again enter into another exclusive songwriting partnership. That experience also taught me that while a handshake contract between friends might give both parties warm and fuzzy feelings, a written contract will prevent a lot of problems later.

Van and I formed a band with Mike Reynolds and Robin Griffin called the Stanbank Production, and our producer, Bud Andrews, arranged for us to demo four of our original tunes at Norman Petty Studios in Clovis, New Mexico. Working with the legendary Norman Petty was an awesome and humbling experience. He was a gracious, gentle, soft-spoken man, and though recording our songs in his studio was intimidating, we were confident they would land us a major label recording and publishing contract. One of the positives that came out of the recording session was that Robin, the drummer in the band, sang the lead vocal on Albuquerque Callin, and on a song he and I wrote called Don't Get Involved. Both had a southern country rock groove, and Robin's bluesy country twang gave the recordings a cool, soulful vibe. I was confident both would become Number One Hits.

There's an old adage in the music business that says the quickest way to break up a band is to have a band photo made, or to record a demo. Indeed, it was only a few months after we did the demos that the band broke up. Albuquerque Callin' was recorded by Nashville artist, Willie Redden, and again by my friend, Johnny James, but neither version made a dent in the charts. Over the years Don't Get Involved remained part of Robin's repertoire in his various bands, as he went on to become a well-known and respected blues rock singer and guitarist in the West Texas area. Mike and Van left the music business.

| AIN'T NOBODY LONELY |

On the road with Jerry Jordan and the Jordan family, we were staying at the Velda Rose Hotel in Hot Springs, Arkansas in the dead of winter. One evening all the Jordan family was invited to a private event, leaving me alone in this once-magnificent hotel, which was now a rundown relic of the glory days of the 1920's. As I stared out the frost-covered window to the cold, empty streets of downtown Hot Springs, I felt at that moment in time that I was the loneliest person in the world. I picked up a pencil and my guitar and scratched out a few lines and a melody. I kept the lyrics with me, and after returning to Lubbock, found them in my guitar case. After a few rewrites, I finished the song, Ain't Nobody Lonely.

Every night, I walk the streets of this lonesome town
Looking for that certain smile, I've waited for so long
I make the bars and the boulevards, till I can't go on
Walkin' home alone I sing, this same old lonesome song:
Ain't nobody lonely, lonely as me,
Ain't nobody knows, ain't nobody sees.
There's got to be someone lonely as me
There's got to be someone, but where can she be?

Ain't Nobody Lonely © 1978, 2010 Cary C. Banks

A few months later my buddy, Johnny James, myself, and some friends, recorded a demo of the song that later found its way onto the Free Whiskey 8-Track album. The Maines Brothers Band recorded the song for the Route 1 Acuff album. The song had become a crowd favorite and was getting some airplay on local radio stations. My friend, Gwen Decker, played it for her friend, Denny Demarco, who was drummer for Rex Allen Jr. Denny loved it and arranged for Don Caldwell and me to meet him in Abilene, Texas to discuss some possible publishing partnerships. Don and I felt quite excited about this Nashville connection, and it appeared some big things might be on the horizon.

Appearances can be deceptive. I developed a fairly close relationship with Denny, and he actively promoted and pitched my songs around Nashville for quite some time. However, though The Maines Brothers Band worked many times with Rex Allen Jr on the West Texas Rehab Telethon, little ever came of that Nashville connection. Eventually, Denny left the music business.

Though Ain't Nobody Lonely has never garnered large financial success or worldwide acclaim, it has become one of the most popular and requested songs of mine. Decades after its first recording, Ryan Castillo, an extremely talented young singer from Elgin, Texas, enrolled at South Plains College as a Commercial Music major. At his first school ensemble audition, he sang Ain't Nobody Lonely.

Later, when quizzed about where he had heard that song, he said, "I was going through a record collection with a buddy in Ropesville, Texas when I came across a Johnny James album called Not Jessie. I heard the song Ain't Nobody Lonely and had an immediate connection with it. I was far from home during my first semester in college, with few people around me, and had become intensely homesick. Like the main character in the song, I walked the streets a lot searching for happiness. Listening to the song made me feel so comfortable, knowing it was okay to be sad, lonely, and homesick. I'm thankful to say the song has gotten me through a lot."

As a writer, you never know where and how far your words will travel, or who it will touch.

| FOOLS LIKE ME |

So raise up your glasses, the drinks are on me.
Come on now, let's strike up the band.
For tonight, we're drinkin' to fools like me,
Who let love slip through their hands.

Fools Like Me © 1978 Cary C. Banks

In the late 1970's I had written a song called Fools like Me that Jack Tyson, Johnny James, and I recorded on an album. We called ourselves the Free Whiskey Band, and our album was released on 8-track tape. Fools Like Me won a quarter-finalist award in the American Song Festival. We won a local Battle of the Bands contest and got to showcase it and a couple of other original songs in a regional Battle of the Bands in Dallas. We didn't win, but an A&R man from a major label was there. He came up to me after the contest and said he was interested in hearing more from us. I spent the next few weeks working on securing a recording contract for the Free Whiskey band. It seemed we were poised for greatness. Jack and Johnny were great singers, and we had just added the phenomenal guitarist, Steve Williams, to the band. We were writing good songs; we sang great

"Fools Like Me" single recorded by Floyd Brown
45rpm single - courtesy Cary Banks Collection

---

harmonies; we drank cheap bourbon whiskey and wore pearl-snap shirts. What could possibly have stood in the way of stardom for us?

We never signed a recording contract, and as often happens in the music business, the band broke up soon after that—and it wasn't because of the pearl-snap shirts. (That's another, not-so-funny story)

Not too long after, Kenny Maines recorded Fools Like Me as a demo. At the time he was lead singer with The Maines Brothers Band, and as part of a demo session at Caldwell studio, sang the vocal on the song. I wasn't present at the session, but the musicians were some of the most prestigious A-list West Texas session players, including: Lloyd Maines, producer and steel guitarist; Larry Welborn, legendary guitarist who played on Buddy Holly's recording of That'll Be the Day; Bill Gamill, pianist, and Curtis McBride, drummer and harmony singer. Kenny did a wonderful job as usual, and I was hopeful something would come of it. Over the years I've been fortunate to have Kenny sing on several of my demos. He always gives a topnotch professional performance. In fact, his vocals were often so good that when I'd pitch my songs to publishers many of them would ask me, "Who's that singer on your demo . . . and does he have a record deal?" They weren't particularly interested in my song, but they were definitely interested in Kenny.

Meanwhile, unbeknownst to me, someone had gotten a copy of Fools Like Me to Nashville songwriter, artist, and producer, John Wesley Ryles. John was a wonderful artist who had a big hit with the song Kay. (Ironically, Kenny had also recorded Kay on one of the earliest Maines Brothers recordings). John Wesley was producing a singer from Baton Rouge, Louisiana named Floyd Brown. Floyd recorded Fools Like Me and a record company in Baton Rouge was prepared to release the song as a single. I received a call one morning from local radio personality, Steve Sever, who worked at the prestigious country station, KLLL. Steve told me some folks in Nashville had contacted him at the radio station wanting to know if he knew the songwriter who owned the rights to Fools like Me.

The song was released and went to Number 1 locally in Baton Rouge. I received a copy of the single, and it was really good. Floyd is a soulful and dynamic singer, and the track, featuring some of Nashville's finest studio players, was fantastic. The beautiful harmony vocals on the cut were sung by a young studio vocalist named Janie Fricke. Janie would go on to have a tremendous solo career, and I would have the honor to play a show with her a few years later.

Okay, here we go again. I settled back and waited for the royalty checks to come in. A short time later I got a call from Floyd Brown himself, who told me he had a falling-out with his record company and was re-releasing the song on his own label. It never received any national attention or recognition, and I didn't hear from Floyd Brown anymore until just recently. I did see him a few years later on the Nashville Network, when he won first place in one of the early TV singing contests called You Can Be a Star. After winning, he went on to co-host a television show called Play It Again Nashville. One of Floyd's co-hosts on the show was legendary country singer, Linda Davis. Floyd would often stay at Linda's home in Nashville and rock her infant daughter, Hillary. Young Hillary (Scott) would grow up in the music business and go on to have an incredibly successful career as lead singer of the superstar group, Lady Antebellum.

During one of the Maines Brothers Band trips to Nashville, I had the opportunity to meet John Wesley Ryles. He was gracious, friendly, and professional, and I thanked him for a wonderful production of my song.

Fools Like Me has been recorded several times, including a single by my friend, Larry Hale. For awhile, Larry owned a little restaurant in Levelland, Texas called Larry's Smokehouse Bar B Q. Larry served great barbeque and also provided a stage where many area musicians would perform. Whenever I played there, I took great delight in introducing Fools Like Me by saying, "Here's my version of a Larry Hale record . . . that I wrote."

| LAY IT DOWN |

Perhaps one of the most painful of my songwriting misadventures happened in 1983. I had officially joined The Maines Brothers Band in January, when keyboardist Randy Brownlow left the band to pursue a more stable and secure career in the oil business. Though I had played with the band many times since 1978, I was now the official piano player and legal member of The Maines Brothers Band LLP Partnership. The band had recorded my songs, Ain't Nobody Lonely and Love Is a Gamble on the Route 1 Acuff album, and Easy to Love on the Panhandle Dancer album. That spring we signed a recording contract with Mercury Records Nashville, and I was Oh So Excited at the prospect of the band recording more of my songs on our first major label album. My songwriting fire burned hotter than ever.

Not long after we had signed our recording contract, I wrote a new song called Lay It Down, a driving country rock style tune with what I thought was a cool storyline and a catchy hook:

Cary Banks of the Maines Brothers Band, whose debut Mercury/Polygram #1 single, "Louisiana Anna" is a hit, is congratulated by Mary Jo Menella, ASCAP membership representative, for winning the 1983 SongSearch competition in the country category for his song, "Lay It Down." Looking on are Barbara Marcus, Executive Director, Songwriters Resources and Services (l) and Carol Banks (r). The awards presentation took place at the 7th Annual Songwriters Expo sponsored by the Los Angeles Songwriters Showcase and SRS.

Photo courtesy - Academy of Country Music

I have been known to drink a little gin.
Stay out late at night, and party with my friends.
I like the way I'm livin' and the crazy things I do,
but I'd lay all that down if you asked me to.

Lay it down, lay it down,
For your sweet love, I'd lay it down

Lay It Down © 1983, 2010 Cary C. Banks

I booked some studio time to make a demo of the song, and Lloyd, Jerry, Donnie, and I laid down a rhythm track while Kenny sang the lead vocal. My friend, Gwen Decker, and I sang some harmony vocals. I thought the demo was pretty cool and sent a copy to my friend, Mark Paden, who was living in Nashville and working as a staff writer for one of the most successful country music publishing companies in the world. A few days later Mark called me and said he had played the demo for some of the songpluggers at the publishing company, and they were really interested in publishing it. Songpluggers are those folks who work for music publishers and their job is to "pitch" the song to artists, producers, TV and Film companies, etc., and try to convince them to record it. He asked if I was willing to sign a publishing agreement for the song, and I couldn't get the words out fast enough . . . YESSSSSSS!!!!!!!!!!!!!!! Wow, look at me! I just signed a major label recording deal, and now I'm being published by one of the world's greatest music publishing companies. My self-importance had just taken a leap into the stratosphere. Yee Haw, here come the royalty checks.

We began working on our first album for Mercury Records with legendary producer, Jerry Kennedy. At Lloyd Maines' insistence, we recorded all the songs at Don Caldwell studios in Lubbock. Mr. Kennedy; Nashville recording engineer, Lou Bradley; and Mercury Records A&R Man, Rick Peoples; flew to Lubbock from Nashville to record and produce the album. As we were choosing songs to record, I pitched Lay It Down as a possibility for the album. Much to my dismay, the band was not excited at all about recording it. At this point in my life, I had been studying, practicing, eating, sleeping, and breathing songwriting for almost fifteen years. I had experienced a little success and lots of failure, but this blow seemed more than I could handle. I had worked so hard and so long, felt like I understood what it took to write a great song, yet here in this moment, I couldn't even get my own band to record what I thought was a sure hit.

An old nagging feeling crept back into my soul that maybe I just wasn't good enough, after all. My frustration and despair over my songwriting career went all the way down to the bone. I kept a journal, kept on writing, but I felt like I was on some never-ending hamster wheel, trying to figure out how to write the next big hit. Every time I thought I had come up with something current, hip, and commercial, in my heart the song rang

> *An old nagging feeling crept back into my soul that maybe I just wasn't good enough, after all. My frustration and despair over my songwriting career went all the way down to the bone.*

hollow and trite. I began to hate the whole process of songwriting and the whole sordid music business.

Ironically, about this same time, on a whim, I entered Lay It Down in a national songwriting contest in California, sponsored by the Los Angeles Song Writers Association and The Songwriters Resources and Services Group. There were several songwriting competitions springing up around that time, and I had won some minor awards with the American Song Festival, so I thought, "Why not? I got nothin' to lose but my thirty dollar entry fee."

A few weeks later I received a call from a young lady named Heidi who worked for the Songwriters Resources and Services group. She asked if I was "the" Cary Banks who had entered a song in the SRS songwriting contest. I said that was me and she excitedly said, "Well, congratulations! Your song, Lay It Down, has won First Place in the Country/Folk division, and we would like to fly you and a guest to Pasadena for the awards ceremony and present you with the one thousand dollar prize." Suddenly, I was not so heartbroken.

Later that month Carol and I flew to California for the awards ceremony and the weekend songwriting workshop. One evening, she and I were walking down the street in downtown Los Angeles when a car full of teenage boys pulled to the curb, doused us both with water, and drove off, laughing hysterically. As we stood there, absolutely soaked, Carol just sighed and said, "Well, welcome to L.A." Other than that, it was a great trip and I got to meet some very influential folks in the music industry.

Meanwhile, Lay It Down appeared to be "laying" dormant on some songpluggers desk at that major publishing company. I began pitching the song myself, anywhere and to anyone I could. I pitched to big acts like Alabama, George Strait, Ronnie Millsap, and countless others. I even pitched it to Ray Charles and hand-delivered it to other artists like Conway Twitty, Moe Bandy, and Ronnie McDowell. I stopped counting after forty-four major label and independent label artists and producers had passed on the song.

One day a producer from South Texas, Darrell Bledsoe, called me to say he had heard a tape of Lay It Down and was sure it was a smash hit. He said he was working with some talented artists and would like to record it. He was confident he could get the song released and promoted as a single, but would need at least a share of the publishing rights. When I told him the song was already assigned to a major publisher, he was disappointed and the fire of his enthusiasm quickly turned to embers. He called back several times after that, asking if I had been able to regain the publishing rights. Sadly, I had to tell him I had not. Eventually, he quit calling.

The folks at the major publishing company had been less than aggressive about promoting the song, and I eventually sent them a registered letter asking for return of my publishing rights. Very rarely does it happen that a songwriter gets the rights back from a publisher, especially since I hadn't insisted on a reversion clause in the original contract. The good folks at the company couldn't even find a copy of the tune, so they graciously and unceremoniously returned the rights back to me. I called my South Texas producer friend and told him I had finally secured the rights to my song, but by then he was no longer interested.

One might assume that after all this time I had gotten over myself and was used to the inevitable rejection inherent in the music industry. In truth, my despair and frustration had gone all the way to the marrow. Lay It Down, which had been published by a major publisher and won first prize in a national song contest, languished unrecorded in my pile of songs for the next twenty-five years. Eventually, I recorded it myself on my CD, A Long Time Since It Rained.

| YOU ARE A MIRACLE |

The summer of 1983 saw The Maines Brothers Band continuing to tour and work on our album. In private, I dealt with my frustration and disappointment as best I could. One afternoon, Jerry Brownlow called and asked if he could come over and show me an idea he had for a ballad he was working on. Jerry had written and sang Break the Fall on the Panhandle Dancer album. To this day, that song remains one of the most

*"You are a Miracle"
single recorded by
Maines Brothers
Band*
*45 rpm single courtesy
- Maines Brothers
collection*

beloved of all the Maines Brothers recordings. For the new song, he had a really cool melody and a lyric hook for a chorus:

> *Like stranded on an island, nowhere to go, no one to talk to,*
> *Nothing there, and no one cared*
> *I thought I'd be there forever, but you appeared like a ship on the water,*
> *Sails so high against the sky*
> *When you heard my lonely cry, you took me away to paradise.*
> *"You are a miracle, oh my miracle, you are a miracle to me"*

© *1983 Cary C. Banks & Jerry Brownlow, Solid Chrome BMI/Turnrow Music ASCAP*

I liked his idea and we began working on verses. I added a piano instrumental intro, and within a couple of hours we had a finished song. At our next band rehearsal, we played it for the group. I must admit that

I was more than a little jaded by this time, and fully expected the band to give us a half-hearted compliment for trying before politely passing on the song. They actually liked it, and we recorded a rough demo in our rehearsal hall. Lloyd sent the tape to Jerry Kennedy and the crew at Mercury, and I once again expected them to pass on it. However, they were excited to record it on our next session and include it on the album. The song was released as our second single on the High Rollin' album, climbed to Number 56 on the charts, and made the first round of Grammy Nominations for Country Song of the Year. It didn't win a Grammy, and climbed no farther on the charts.

In another bittersweet moment The Maines Brothers Band had our picture in People magazine—YEE HAW—but the review panned You Are a Miracle as "too treacly." As they say out here in West Texas, "You take the shit with the sugar." My self-importance once again came crashing down out of the stratosphere.

The Maines Brothers Band recorded a second album on Mercury Records called The Boys are Back in Town. This album featured the song Everybody Needs Love on a Saturday Night, which made it to the Top Twenty on the Billboard Country Charts. We spent the next two years burning up the highway from California to New York, promoting the album and trying to establish ourselves as a national act. None of my songs were recorded on the album. I would like to say I accepted that graciously and without despair and resentment. I did not.

Songs are little gifts from the musical universe, and you are truly blessed if you are given a good one.

Over the many years of my songwriting journey, I learned a lot of tough lessons and hard truths. The basics of songwriting, i.e. rhyming, song form, melody, and rhythm are fairly straight-forward and most anyone can learn them. However, as I stated earlier, a really good song is incredibly hard to write, and writing a great song is next-to-impossible. Songs are little gifts from the musical universe, and you are truly blessed if you are given a good one.

During the decade of the '80's, my songwriting career was a series of great expectations and shattered dreams, with many a dark night of the soul. It was a heartbreaking and lonely time of brooding self-doubt tempered with a deep-down knowing that I truly loved playing music and writing songs, and I would never stop doing either, no matter where the path of my career would take me. I think my friend, Bonnie Bishop, captured the essence of the double-edged sword of the loneliness of the heartbroken songwriter with her song, The Best Songs Come from Broken Hearts.

ALL WE GOT IS DR PEPPER

Our first Maines Brothers Band gig, at the original Antone's in Austin, was opening a show for a giant superstar in the Texas Music scene. We had arrived earlier in the afternoon, set up and had our sound check, and were just chillin' in the small dressing room just off to the side of the stage. We saw the giant superstar's tour bus pull up to the venue, and watched as this larger-than-life character walked into the little dressing room. An established legend who literally took over any room he entered, he looked around, smiled, and proclaimed in a deep bass voice, "SO . . . this is the famous MAINES BROTHERS BAND. Where's the coke?" To which Jerry, in all naïve sincerity replied, "Sorry man, all we got is Dr Pepper."

The look on the star's face was complete bemused bewilderment. He stared at Jerry a moment, shook his head, and mumbled something under his breath as he turned to walk up to the stage.

Over the years, we played several other shows with this Texas Music Icon but I don't remember him ever asking about our backstage accoutrements again.

ALL THE MONEY IN MY LIFE

With the growing success of our new single, Everybody Needs Love on a Saturday Night, we signed a management/booking agreement with Barbara Mandrell's Booking Agency. Barbara had not performed publicly since her horrible car accident a couple of years before, but was now feeling well enough to embark on a new tour, and The Maines Brothers Band was chosen as her opening act. We traveled literally from coast to coast and found ourselves in Cleveland, Ohio, with a rare day without a scheduled show. Jerry Brownlow, our self-proclaimed gambling expert, suggested we go to the racetrack and win ourselves a little extra spending cash. Although my uncle and some great-uncles owned race horses in New Mexico, I had never been to a professional track. I figured with Jerry's expertise and my limited funds, what did I have to lose? We spent the day with him coaching us on how to bet the odds.

When the last race of the day came up, Jerry was up in winnings while the rest of us were doing good to break even. Several of us decided to place our last bets on Number 11. He had the best odds to at least show, and his jockey had a winning track record. I must admit the whole process was quite exciting and entertaining, and we were all whoopin' and hollerin' as the starting gate flew open. Despite our enthusiasm and encouragement, I don't know if Number 11 has crossed the finish line to this day. Oh well, we were drinking beer and having a good time anyway.

> *I must admit the whole process was quite exciting and entertaining, and we were all whoopin' and hollerin' as the starting gate flew open.*

We had spent the whole afternoon partying, and some of us decided to go to a local club and continue our day-off celebration. I don't remember how we got there, but we met an Irishman at the club who insisted on buying us drinks—all except Donnie who always remained our sober caretaker. The celebration continued until the Irishman ran out of money. At that point, Jerry decided he would bankroll the remainder of the evening with his racetrack winnings. I don't remember how long we stayed, but thanks to the grace and watchful eye of Donnie Maines, we somehow found our way back to the motel.

In an effort to remain fiscally responsible and frugal on the road, Brother Steve Maines would often book as few motel rooms as possible, which meant we often had to share a bed with a fellow band member. This was nothing new to me, as my younger brothers, Russ and Jake, and I had often slept three to a bed. The Maines Brothers Band caveat was that one person would sleep under the sheets and one on top of them; i.e. No Skin Touching. That particular night I was sharing a bed with Lloyd Maines. By the time I got to the room it was dark, and it appeared that Lloyd had already drifted off to sleep. As quietly as a mouse, I got undressed and gingerly slipped in on my side (on top of the covers, of course). Apparently, I must have caught Lloyd in the middle of a violent dream, because no sooner had my head hit the pillow than he literally kicked me out of bed.

With a resounding thud, I landed on the motel floor like a hundred-pound sack of flour. My immediate response was hysterical laughter, which of course woke him. With one eye half-open, he looked at me on the floor, said "Sorry, man," and immediately went back to sleep. As I lay there trying to stifle my laughter, I thought what a poetically perfect ending to a hard day's night.

The next morning, Jerry was sitting on the edge of his bed, forlornly gazing into his empty wallet.

"What's wrong, man?" someone asked.

Jerry hung his head in despair. "I think I spent all the money in my life last night."

ARE WE ABOUT TO HAVE AN ATTITUDE CONTEST HERE?

We were playing an outdoor festival in Wichita Falls, Texas with the Fabulous Thunderbirds, The Beach Boys, and a couple of other bands. We had spent the night before in a local motel and arrived at the event at our scheduled time. Evidently, the schedule had been changed, and the promoters had sent a message to our hotel, but it had never been delivered to us.

Backstage passes for concert in Wichita Falls Texas Featuring The Beach Boys, The Fabulous Thunderbirds, The Maines Brothers Band
Backstage passes courtesy - Joe Piland

As we got to the entrance gate of the festival, a brash young guy, evidently employed by the concert promoters as some kind of backstage manager, sporting a Satin Tour Jacket (very popular at the time), came up to our vehicle and began yelling insults at us for being late and unprofessional. His obviously arrogant attitude suggested he thought of us as a bunch of hayseed rednecks from Lubbock. When Lloyd Maines showed him the schedule we had been given the night before by the promoters, and tried to explain that no one had notified us of the changes, the man became more obnoxious and more determined to show us he was in charge and might not even let us in.

Now, all of Lloyd's family, friends, and associates know him as a gentle giant with a friendly smile and sweet spirit, but those who meet him for the first time are immediately struck by his tall, broad-shouldered appearance and commanding voice. In fact, some even assume he's a professional athlete. Lloyd calmly looked at the man and said, "Are we about to have an attitude contest here?"

All of us in the van sat silently watching this fascinating interchange, wondering what was coming next. The young gatekeeper immediately began backing off, stammering something about how we should have double-checked the schedule. I looked at him, still pitifully trying to project his macho image, and saw a hint of fear in his eyes.

"Okay, just hurry and get set up; we're behind schedule," he lamely ended.

I had to smile as I realized he had figured out that Lloyd had a Ph.D. in attitude and was about to hang it on that young man's wall.

The show was great, and I really enjoyed hearing the Beach Boys, who were some of my early musical heroes. Lesson for the day: "You Don't Mess With Texas and You Don't Mess With Lloyd Maines." I don't care how many official badges you have on your Satin Tour Jacket.

DON'T SHOOT ME, I'M JUST THE BASS PLAYER

There is an old adage in show business that says, "No matter what happens, the show must go on." There are countless stories of singers and guitarists falling off the front of the stage, or drummers falling off the back of it, and numerous other accidents. Legendary blues guitarist, Jesse Taylor, once received a severe electric shock when he was touching the strings of his guitar, and reached over to grab an ungrounded electric tuner. He was seriously shocked, but finished the show. During one of the infamous Tornado Jam concerts in Lubbock, a sudden rainstorm flooded the outdoor stage while Lloyd Maines was playing his pedal steel guitar. The rain was so fast and furious that Lloyd looked down to see his fingerpicks floating in water in the space between the two necks of the instrument. Undaunted, he kept right on playing.

One particular moment stands out during The Maines Brothers Band's performance at the Civic Center Banquet Hall in Lubbock. We were right in the middle of our version of Bob Seger's hard-driving Betty Lou's Getting Out Tonight. The dancers were having a great time, and the audience was singing along, when suddenly I heard a crash and the sound of open bass strings ringing and rumbling out-of-tune and out-of-time. I looked over to see Jerry Brownlow, fallen on his back, ferociously pounding his right knee while attempting to find the notes on his bass with his left hand. Behind the audience at the back of the room, both sound man Joe Piland and guest, Terry Allen, thought Jerry had been shot. Terry raced to the stage as Steve Maines was attempting to help Jerry back to his feet. Unbeknownst to the rest of us, his knee had suddenly popped out of joint, and he was frantically trying to pound it back in place. He waved off Steve and Terry, and we finished the song with Jerry sitting on the floor.

Jerry's comment: "I think I twisted my nervous."

DUDE . . . IT'S JUST A TELETHON

For several years The Maines Brothers Band had the honor of performing as both featured artists and the country stage band for the West Texas Rehab Telethon filmed in Abilene, Texas. As the stage band, we had the glorious opportunity to work with such notable entertainers as Janie Frickie, Lee Ann Rimes, Rex Allen Sr., Rex Allen Jr., Lee Roy Parnell, Steve Wariner, Brad Maul, Connie Smith, Rob Roy Parnell, and many others.

The Maines Brothers Band with our tour bus for an album photo shoot in front of the legendary "Lindsey Theater" in downtown Lubbock Texas
Photo courtesy - Matt Barnes

Rex Allen Jr. was a regular host of the program, and during one particular show his drummer, Denny Demarco, was serving as stage manager. A talented up-and-coming rock band from Lubbock, The Nelsons, featuring Donnie Allison and John Sprott, were guest performers on the telethon. The show generally featured only pop, swing, and country artists, and this was a first one to have rock and roll entertainers. Sound check hadn't gone very well, and since the event would be seen by thousands of viewers over dozens of ABC Television affiliates throughout West and Central Texas and southern Oklahoma, the guys in The Nelsons were nervous about their performance. They kept coming to Denny with concerns about monitor placement, volume levels, etc. until finally Denny, by this time becoming annoyed, said to one of the band members, "Dude, chill out. It's just a telethon."

That was one of the many situations that taught me how to love live TV and how to keep the entertainment business in perspective.

That particular telethon, The Maines Brothers Band had driven to Abilene in our newly-purchased Silver Eagle touring bus, with the '57 Chevy murals painted on the sides and back. The Nelsons' guitarist, John Sprott, remembers that his band had limped in to Abilene that evening in their 1976 Ford Econoline van that was on its third transmission. They had barely made it into the parking lot of the venue when it was determined the van would have to be towed to a local auto shop for more repairs before it was deemed roadworthy again. John recalls that he and the telethon's headliner, a young Wynonna Judd, were standing together looking out a window at The Maines Brothers Band bus. Wynonna, observing The Nelsons with their rockabilly hairdo's and wild '80's punk rock/new wave outfits, asked John if that was his band's bus. With all bravado humbly put aside, John answered, "No, that's our white Econoline van behind that tow truck." Spoken like a true rock star.

The Nelsons did a fabulous job on the telethon that evening, and it wasn't long after that the group gained national popularity and attention when their video, I Don't Mind, was featured on the MTV Basement Tapes television show.

MAN, THIS IS NOT AN ARRANGEMENT

On our second Mercury Records album, The Maines Brothers Band recorded a song by the Bus Boys, from the movie 48 Hours, called The Boys are Back in Town. Our recording featured Richard Bowden playing trumpet and some other local horn players, including Don Caldwell on tenor sax and Tommy Anderson on trumpet, playing a rock/R&B style horn arrangement. When we were invited to perform the song on the Nashville Now television show, we wanted the Nashville Now horn players to play with us.

Over the years I had taught myself to write charts with simple horn or string arrangements by working with horn players and by watching friends like Bill Gammill do arrangements for recording sessions at Don Caldwell studio, although I could never make my charts look as neat and pretty as Bill's. So, on the tour bus ride all the way from Lubbock to Nashville, I labored to write horn arrangements for our song for the Nashville Now horn section: two trumpets, two saxophones, and a trombone. Not having access to a copy machine, I meticulously hand-copied five complete arrangements for the song.

Maines Brothers Band performing of Nashville Now TV show with Nashville Now horn players
Photo courtesy - TNN/ Nashville Now/ Greg Cook

When we got to the set for our rehearsal, eager to show off my arranging talents, I proudly approached the band leader of the horn section, told him we would like for him and his horn players to play with us on the show, and showed him my glorious arrangement.

Taking one look at it, he said, "Man, this is not an arrangement, this is a damn career." He smiled at me and handed back the charts. "Thanks, but a couple of us will do a little head arrangement during your sound check." (They would make up their parts by ear) I was both flattered by his compliment on my arranging abilities, and pissed I had put in so much time and effort, and they weren't even going to look at the arrangements. The guys were superb, professional musicians who could read quite well but were also great ear players. We did the show, and of course the horn section sounded great.

CASCADE AND DOG FOOD

One of the most interesting characters I have ever had the privilege to work with is Richard Ashley Bowden. Richard is one of the most energetic and creative musicians I've ever known. He is a master fiddler and mandolinist, good singer, and plays a pretty mean trumpet as well. He's also the only person I know personally who was actually at the Woodstock Music Festival in 1969. He and his family were living in New York at that time, and he and a buddy hitchhiked all the way to Max Yasgur's farm in upstate New York to be part of that momentous, once-in-a-lifetime event.

Richard is his own person. A true rock and roll gypsy at heart, he has traveled the world, played with a host of disparate artists such as Boxcar Willie, the Austin Lounge Lizards, Ryan Bingham and others. He is intelligent, incredibly talented and musical, politically active—he helped establish and continues to promote the Million Musicians March for Peace—and a fine man with a sensitive and gentle soul.

Anyone who has spent time on a tour bus understands how the monotony of mile after mile of highway can take its toll on your mind, body,

Maines Brothers Band at Kerrville Folk Festival
Photo courtesy - Maines Brothers Collection

and spirit. There's an old saying that life on the road means: "You don't eat right, don't sleep right, don't crap right." A Silver Eagle tour bus with seven musicians, a sound man, a lighting guy, and a bus driver will certainly test a man's patience even in the best of situations.

One particular night, somewhere in southeast Alabama, we had stopped at some tired-old truck stop along the highway at four in the morning to gas up. Those of us who were still awake decided to stretch our legs and see what kind of junk food we could find. After filling the enormous diesel tank, loading ourselves down with Cheetos, beef jerky, Hershey bars, and oatmeal cookies, we got back aboard and started out of the parking lot. Suddenly, someone who was mostly awake and aware at this ungodly hour, said "Hey, anybody see Richard get back on the bus?"

We looked around, checked all the sleeping bunks and couldn't find a trace of him. This was not an uncommon occurrence. Often times when we would stop, Richard would take the opportunity to get some exercise and strike out jogging down the highway. More than once we had taken off from our rest stop and found him a mile or so up the road. This time, one of us decided to go back in the truck stop to check for him. Sure enough, there he was, wandering the grocery aisles, checking prices and ingredients on the packages of Cascade dish soap and Purina dog food.

I'm not sure what use that information would have been to us on the bus, but should the need ever arise, Richard would be our go-to source.

If you've ever witnessed a Maines Brothers Band performance, doubtless one of the images that will linger in your memory is the band blistering its way through New Delhi Freight Train, with Lloyd Maines absolutely burning up the steel guitar while Richard Bowden hovers over him, standing on Lloyd's stool, sawing on the fiddle like his hair was on fire.

HOW LONG'S IT TAKE YOU TO PACK UP 'EM DRUMS, ANYWAY?

One of the first things you learn as a professional musician playing in bars is: Never argue with or try to explain yourself to a drunk."

We had just finished our show at a honky-tonk somewhere in Texas, and Donnie Maines had begun the long and tedious process of packing up his drums, cymbals, stands, and hardware into cases and loading them into our equipment trailer. I noticed this drunk cowboy staggering around, spilling what was left of his beer and staring intently at Donnie. The more he stared, the more frustrated and impatient he seemed to be. Finally, he couldn't take it anymore, and stumbled over and spouted, "How long's it take you to pack up 'em drums anyway?

Donnie just looked at him, smiled and said, "About an hour . . . two if I got help."

GUN CONTROL

Being a collection of Alpha males, The Maines Brothers Band and several of our friends would, from time to time, gather together for a little fishing or hunting experience. Don Caldwell, Tommy Anderson, Bob Hudnal, and others would sometimes join us on these treks to the wild. I missed the particular fishing expedition where Don Caldwell sank his boat; or the time the boat came off the trailer and stuck itself, bow first, into the dirt road leading from the lake to the highway. The boat stories have grown exponentially over the years, but I can't really verify them. I've never been much of a fisherman, and I'm certainly not skilled as a hunter. In fact, the animals feel quite safe when I'm around.

After a late night gig in Amarillo, some of the guys had planned a hunting trip for the next morning to shoot Sandhill crane. It was early spring, and the weather in West Texas can be brutal that time of year. It was especially cold and windy that evening.

According to the experts, the way to hunt cranes is to travel to an open field before the sun comes up. Once there, you find a place to lie on your back, sometimes for hours, your shotgun at your side, and wait for the giant flock to fly overhead. Once they are directly above you, you open fire and try to get off as many shots as possible before the birds fly away.

Several of the guys had brought their shotguns with them on the bus, planning to go to the hunting field as soon as we unloaded all our music gear back in Lubbock around five o'clock in the morning. The avid hunters were doing their best to cajole and coerce us non-hunters to join them in this little adventure. "Come on, man; it'll be lots of fun," or "Don't be such a wuss," were some of the taunts thrown at us. Finally, after the good-natured mockery had reached a point of absurdity, Kenny Maines sarcastically remarked, "Yeah, that's my idea of a good time. Hanging around in the cold with a bunch of guys who are tired, hungry, hungover, pissed off . . . and carryin' guns."

> *"Yeah, that's my idea of a good time. Hanging around in the cold with a bunch of guys who are tired, hungry, hungover, pissed off . . . and carryin' guns."*

And now, to paraphrase the legendary radio personality, Paul Harvey, here's "The Rest of the Story:"

That particular morning, Donnie Maines and our bus driver, Brad Thompson, were part of the hunting party that traveled to a wildlife preserve just outside of Muleshoe, Texas. The hunters arrived before dawn, dressed in warm long johns, heavy jeans, insulated coveralls, and thick boots. For added protection from the cold, some of the guys offered Donnie and Brad some patented "gun oil" (Crown Royal Whiskey). Donnie politely declined, and he and Brad found a spot just outside the fence boundary of the wildlife preserve to assume their strategic positions. On this particular preserve there were several salt playa lakes where the Sandhill cranes gathered that time of year. Every morning just after daybreak, hundreds of them would take to the skies from the playa lakes like a thunderous battalion of B-52's. I'm told the sound is almost deafening.

As the first wave of birds took flight over the hunters, Donnie got off a shot which appeared to hit one of them. The bird spiraled to the ground and folded up like a cheap tent inside the fenced area of the wildlife preserve. It is illegal in Texas to carry a firearm onto a state wildlife preserve, so Donnie and Brad left their shotguns at the edge of the fence and crawled through the barbed wire to retrieve the crane. As they got to a position just a few feet away from the bird, it suddenly stood up, spread its massive wings like a Japanese ninja, and looked as if it was about to attack the two hunters.

Brad began running his hand over the fabric on his arms, and when Donnie asked what he was doing, he replied, "Do you think that big old beak of his can peck through these insulated overalls?" There they were, out in the middle of a barren field, not sure if they were the hunter or the hunted, when Donnie spotted a dried cow pattie on the ground by his feet. In an act of extreme creative bravery (or blatant self-preservation), he picked up the dried feces, and like a major league baseball pitcher, chunked it as hard as he could at the menacing bird. It landed squarely on its throat, and the crane once again crumbled to the ground. At that point, Brad and Donnie subdued the dead animal and proceeded to take it back to the truck.

And that's how the legend was born of the fearless Donnie Maines, who took out the giant threatening Sandhill crane with his infamous assault turd.

SINGIN' IN A CHOIR WITH TONY DORSETT AND OLIVE OYL

In January 1985, after the American Music Awards in Hollywood, a giant gang of rock, country, R&B and Pop stars gathered at a recording studio to be part of the video that would become the biggest musical event of the entire year: We Are the World, a song written by Lionel Richie and Michael Jackson, and produced by Quincy Jones. The purpose of this colossal project was to bring awareness to, and raise money for food for, starving multitudes in Africa. A single of the song was recorded, a video was created, and a documentary video was produced of the making of the video. Featured stars included Bruce Springsteen, Bob Dylan, Stevie Wonder, Kenny Rogers, and virtually anyone that was anyone in the mid'80's music world. In fact someone at the event was overheard to say something along the lines of "If an atom bomb were to hit this building tonight, John Denver would be back on top of the music business." MTV was all the rage at that point, and you simply could not go anywhere in the world at any given time of the day and not see or hear We Are the World.

As usual, the Great State of Texas was not to be outdone. A state organization commissioned some Texas songwriters to compose an epic anthem called Here is My Love, that would be similar in style to We Are the World. The organization then put together a massive event called the Texas World Reunion for Hunger Relief in Texas and Africa. The event brought together Texas musicians, entertainers,

Texas celebrities gathered together to make a record and video - "Here is our Love"
Photo courtesy - Joe Piland

actors, athletes, and other types of celebrities with a connection to Texas. They gathered at the Las Colinas Entertainment Complex in Dallas to participate in the filming of the video for Here Is Our Love.

The Maines Brothers Band was invited to participate, along with other Texas Music artists, including the Gatlin Brothers, Rusty Weir, B. J. Thomas, Trini Lopez, Alex Harvey, Billy Preston, Charlie Pride, Steven Stills, Mary Wilson, and a host of others. Celebrity athletes like Roger Staubach, Mean Joe Green, Martina Navratilova, Tony Dorsett, and Earl Campbell; and actors such as Shelley Duvall (Olive Oyl in the Popeye movie), Katherine Helmond, Lee Horsley and child actor, Henry Thomas of ET fame, were also part of the giant gala event.

We arrived at Las Colinas around five o'clock that evening for pre-taping drinks and hors d' oeuvres. (In Texas we call 'em chicken wings and cheese dip). To say the wine and liquor were flowing in abundance would be a huge understatement, and we were all taking full advantage of FREE food and drink. It was a surreal experience seeing all these celebrities in one place. Of course, we had our pictures taken with as many celebrities as possible. At one point, superstar running back Earl Campbell asked Lloyd Maines what team he played for. I'm pretty sure I heard Lloyd tell that story at least five times that night. Later in the evening, after a few margaritas, Lloyd looked across the room at Earl and jokingly proclaimed, "I think just one more margarita and I could take him."

The filming of the song was supposed to start around 7:30 that evening, but it was past eleven before we were herded into a large studio and assigned positions on a giant set of four-tiered choir risers. At that point, it was a wonder any of us could even walk, much less climb up on a bunch of shaky risers.

Around midnight, this giant choir of celebrities finally began singing along with the track of Here Is My Love. There must have been more than a hundred of us crowded onto those risers in that impromptu choir, all in a festive spirit, no pun intended. I was standing near the Gatlin Brothers, who were cracking up everyone with their nonstop humor. Everywhere I looked the celebrities appeared to be having a great time singin', swayin', and holdin' hands.

After the taping some of us gathered in the parking lot and watched in amazement as Earl Campbell commandeered one of the limousines, climbed into the driver's seat, and drove off across the grounds of the Las Colinas Complex while the limo driver stood in stunned silence.

There was a single of the song released, and some video footage of the taping was shown on various Texas TV networks. A Youtube video still floats around the internet. I don't recall hearing if the project successfully raised any money for the hungry, but we had a heck of a good time recording it.

The best quote of the night came from Jerry Brownlow, who said, "I never dreamed I'd be singin' in a choir and holdin' hands with Tony Dorsett and Olive Oyl."

THE TEXAS CONNECTION AND THE CUSSIN' SONGS

Many of my wife, Carol's, relatives had never had the opportunity to see The Maines Brothers Band, and were very excited to watch our performance on the Texas Connection Television Show, hosted by Jerry Jeff Walker on the Nashville Network Cable Channel. The show was filmed in the same location as the original Austin City Limits, but featured a different backdrop and stage design. My father-in-law, Reverend Earl Harvey, and mother-in-law, Vivian, were big fans of The Maines Brothers Band, and had bragged to their friends and relatives that we were talented and wholesome young men with songs everyone would surely enjoy.

On that particular show we had decided to perform a couple of our

Backstage pass for the Texas Connection TV show
Backstage pass courtesy - Joe Piland

more popular Texas songs, including Texas Tears, written by Terry Allen, which featured a couple of blaringly blatant "damn you" lyrics, and You Can't Get the Hell Out of Texas, written by John Hadley, which boasts about the "hell-raisin'" nature of the great state of Texas.

After the broadcast, my father-in-law half-jokingly said, "Well, we finally got our relatives and friends and church members to tune-in and see your band, and all you did was cussin' songs."

The most memorable moment of that evening was sitting backstage listening to the famous Guy Clark tell hilarious stories about his friend, Townes Van Zandt. I was particularly intrigued by the tale of Townes' depressing but oddly humorous visit to a psychiatrist, a story that was the inspiration for a song Guy wrote titled, Doctor, Good Doctor. What an honor it was to be in the presence and hear the yarns of such a gifted tunesmith.

HOLDING COUNTRY MUSIC IN MY ARMS

Years ago, Rolling Stone magazine stated that, early in their career, ZZ Top played a three hour show at some out-of-the-way venue in south Texas for one guy who had paid his admission. The story has become legendary, and I've often told it when asked what it's like to play for an empty house, or a hostile or even apathetic audience. I've also been asked what it's like to play for thousands of screaming fans. It's interesting that in both cases the feelings can be quite similar. I learned early-on in my career that there is a symbiotic relationship between performer and audience, and both are equally important. One draws energy from the other; one feeds the other, and both create this wonderful synergy that is hard to describe. If you understand that relationship, love the fact that you are privileged to be a part of it, and want to give the other your very best, it's a joy and wonder that can scarcely be explained. It just has to be experienced.

My first gig was with my friend, Danny Johnson. I had just started playing guitar, and he and I had worked up a few Beatles tunes with him

★ After playing their hearts out, the **Maines Brothers Band** joined in on the historic grand finale to the sizzling Mercury/Polygram show at Fan Fair in June. Included in the line-up above you can find all seven of our guys plus such notables as **Tom T. Hall, Jerry Lee Lewis, Donna Fargo, Johnny Cash, Johnny Paycheck, Frank Yankovic, Carl Perkins, Glenn Sutton, and Lynn Anderson.** Off stage our time was spent doing what is really at the heart of Fan Fair: signing autographs. For us it's really a great chance to get to talk to the individuals who like the Maines Brothers Band sound. Both on stage and off, it was a great few days. photo by Alan Mayor

Photo courtesy- Alan Mayor

---

singing lead and me playing guitar and singing harmony. My dad was teaching auto mechanics at Howard College in Big Spring. His small class had graduated, and he was throwing them a dinner party at a local Mexican restaurant. He asked if Danny and I would sing a few songs at the celebration. Though we had some experience performing in choir together, we had never had this kind of up-close-and-personal gig. I remember we were pretty nervous, and when we sang the Beatles song, Misery, my mom said she almost laughed out loud, because we looked as though we were indeed miserable.

From that incident, I learned a valuable show biz lesson that would stay with me my entire life: the audience listens with their eyes. From that point on, I tried to imagine what they were experiencing when I was on stage. I thoroughly loved being on stage and playing music, but I had to make sure the audience was seeing and feeling the joy I was feeling. That wasn't always easy. I got a taste of barroom crowd-mentality the first time I ever played a honky-tonk. We were setting up the PA system and speaking into the microphones the obligatory "Mic Test, Mic Test, 1, 2 3," when an inebriated patron from the back of the bar yelled, "Mike's drunk!" followed by raucous laughter and continual heckling from the already-tipsy crowd. The night pretty much went downhill from there.

Over the years I've had the privilege of performing at some spectacular events on giant stages in front of thousands of people. Back in the 1980's, before what is now known as the Austin City Limits Music Festival, The Maines Brothers Band often performed at a giant festival known as Aqua Fest in downtown Austin, on the banks of what was then called Town Lake. (The lake has since been renamed Lady Bird Lake in honor of Lady Bird Johnson.)

One particular performance, the lineup featured our band, Kris Kristofferson, Tanya Tucker, Billy Swan, and blues legend, Albert Collins. I remember being on stage looking out into the crowd of cheering fans and not being able to see the end of the audience. I don't know the exact number of people in attendance that evening, but the sea of souls seemed to stretch from the front of the stage to the edge of the horizon and beyond. I had never performed in front of a crowd that size, and the moment took on an air of the surreal. It was, at one and the same time, an exhilarating feeling, and a feeling of disconnection. The thought occurred to me that if I can't see the end of the crowd, can they even see me?

The thought occurred to me that if I can't see the end of the crowd, can they even see me?

A full color photo of the event appeared on the front page of the Austin Statesman newspaper the next day, taken from somewhere in the back of the enormous expanse of bodies. I recognized the tiny red dot on the stage as the red t-shirt I had been wearing.

For many performers, when you are in front of a large crowd like that, the tendency is to play louder, harder, and more intensely than normal. Of course, that was also back in the day before "in ear" monitor systems, when the onstage monitor wedges were often pumping out decibels rivaled only by a jet engine, and the volume philosophy was basically "everything louder than everything else." For our band, it was the glorious explosion of the emotional, physical, mental, and spiritual energy of seven guys giving everything we had to the moment. We loved it, and we tried to capture that same intensity in every performance.

I have been asked to describe the feeling of performing in front of thousands of screaming fans, and the only way I can do so is to say that it is like being in love with twenty-thousand people you've never met.

Drummer Royce Glen said it best: "The ticketholder is the boss, and it's my job on stage to make sure they get their money's worth."

For me, one of the most memorable performances was when The Maines Brothers Band performed at the Mercury Records Showcase Stage at Country Music Fan Fair Festival in Nashville, Tennessee in June of 1985. The event was held at the racetrack in Nashville, and each Mercury artist had a short, fifteen-minute showcase during the afternoon. Tom T. Hall was the emcee, and at the end, all the artists were brought up on stage for a grand finale of Will the Circle Be Unbroken. There we were, singing with Tom T. Hall and his wife, Dixie, Johnny Cash, Jerry Lee Lewis, Carl Perkins and his band, Kathy Mattea, Johnny Paycheck, Mentor Williams, Donna Fargo, and a Holy Host of other singers and pickers. A CMA magazine posted the photo years later, and I was able to keep a copy that I absolutely treasure.

After the show there was a photographer backstage who saw some of us talking with rising star, Kathy Mattea, and urged us to gather round for a photo-op. He encouraged us to look like we were having a great time, and to do something crazy. I'm not sure what possessed me to take his suggestion, but at the very instant he snapped the picture, I reached over and swooped Kathy Mattea into my arms as though I was carrying her over a threshold. She was gracious and good-natured about the whole incident, but looking back, it's a wonder she didn't slap the crap out of me. Somewhere, in some forgotten country music magazine from 1985, is a picture of me holding Kathy Mattea in my arms.

WHEN HE CAME TO HIMSELF

In the New Testament book of Luke, Chapter 15, is the parable of the prodigal son. Most folks are familiar with the story of the young man who demands his inheritance from his father and then travels off to a far country and wastes all his money on wine, women, and song. When the money runs out and his good-time friends are all gone, he finds himself alone and destitute, working as an indentured servant slopping pigs, so hungry he wishes he could eat the slop he's feeding them. In verses 17 and 18, it reads, (I paraphrase) "and when he came to himself, he said . . . I will arise and go to my father and say unto him, 'Father, I have sinned against heaven and before thee and am no longer worthy to be called thy son; make me as one of thy hired servants.'"

My descent into decadence had been gradual, and my redemption would be similar. Year after year my mom and dad continued to pray for my repentance, and my father and mother-in-law were gracious and patient with me, never forcing their beliefs on me. They simply lived and proclaimed their faith daily by their words and actions. Gradually, I softened my death-grip against religion and began to seriously listen and observe. In 1980, I actually wrote a gospel tune called Sing a Song for Jesus that was recorded by my friend, the singing farmer from Petersburg, Jim Fullingim. He even named titled his album after my song title.

I still wasn't completely on-board the gospel train and was leery of fundamentalist preaching and doctrines, but I was beginning to see that my view of life and reality was more and more suspect. The more I tried to control my life, my circumstances, and my career, the more it slipped out of my grasp.

> *The more I tried to control my life, my circumstances, and my career, the more it slipped out of my grasp.*

Toward the end of the 1980's, The Maines Brothers Band dissolved our deal with Mercury Records. Additionally, the once-prosperous West Texas oil field business turned from boom to bust, and the legal drinking age in Texas changed from nineteen-years-old to twenty-one. Many of the clubs we played began to close their doors. The band found itself saddled with the debt of owning a tour bus while trying to generate enough income to support eight families with an ever-dwindling number of performance venues. My songwriting output had gone from anemic to barely breathing. Personal and band morale was, to say the least, less than enthusiastic. Still, we kept plugging away, always giving 100% and putting on the best show we possibly could.

All the years of bad eating habits, millions of miles of traveling in moving vehicles, and toting around heavy musical instruments had taken its toll on my body, especially my elimination system. I had developed a case of hemorrhoids so serious it required surgery. It seemed that a big part of my career had become a giant pain in the ass.

All these factors seemed to come together to create a perfect spiritual storm. One night, as I was approaching my thirty-eighth birthday, I couldn't sleep. It seemed I had reached some kind of pivotal moment. All the family was asleep, but I lay there spiritually broken, emotionally out-of-gas, and creatively bankrupt. I sensed that my spiritual life lacked any real integrity. In a moment of desperation, I called out to God, "Lord, I can't go on like this. I have no more answers, no more strength, and no hope for my future. I give up. I give it all to you, Lord. Take my life and do with it what you will. I surrender."

There was no Damascus road experience with a blinding light, or a holy host of angels, or a thunderous voice from God, but as I lay there, emotionally spent and mentally helpless, I sensed a new peace in my spirit. A peace I couldn't fully understand or describe. (Philippians 4:7: "And the peace of God that passes all understanding shall keep your hearts and minds through Jesus Christ.") The truth of this Jesus, a truth I had been denying and avoiding all those years, was now so true to me that I had no words to describe it. I only knew that I knew that I knew.

My transformation was not immediate or grandiose, but I sensed that my life would never be the same. My problems were not immediately solved; in fact, many of them became worse. I still had a lot of questions, doubts, and insecurities, but I no longer felt a sense of despair and hopelessness. For Carol and me, the next few years saw hard financial times, my mother-in-law's heartbreaking illness and death, and the challenges of raising two bright, but strong-willed children. I didn't realize that slow and subtle, but profound changes were happening in my life. Sometimes I couldn't figure out if I had made a great and wonderful decision to surrender my life and will to God, or if I had taken the coward's way out and just given up and quit trying. I'm still amazed at how hard it is for so many of us to understand the concept and accept the free gift of grace. Years later, my friend, Matt Smith, would describe what I was feeling in a most humorous and profound way. "The problem with surrendering your will and giving all your problems to God is, He acts like He has all the time in the world."

From the moment after that sleepless night, at the core of my being I needed and longed to have that closer walk with Jesus, and to know Him and His word deeper and stronger than ever. He most assuredly met me in my need. As the old adage says, "What once was my mess has now become my message."

My transformation was not immediate or grandiose, but I sensed that my life would never be the same. My problems were not immediately solved; in fact, many of them became worse. I still had a lot of questions, doubts, and insecurities, but I no longer felt a sense of despair and hopelessness.

"But when he was yet a great way off, his father saw him, and had compassion, and ran, and fell on his neck and kissed him . . . and said to his servants, "Bring forth the best robe and put it on him; and put a ring on his hand and shoes on his feet . . . for this my son was dead, and is alive again; he was lost, and is found." (Luke 15: 20-24)

Art designed by Terry Allen
Photo courtesy - Shonda Crutchfield Photography

part five

THE ONLY MOUNTAIN IN LUBBOCK

"If you can't fix it . . . feature it."

- Dr. Jerry Goolsby

THE ONLY MOUNTAIN IN LUBBOCK

In 1971 I was fortunate to record in the legendary Norman Petty recording studio in Clovis, New Mexico. While it was a tremendous thrill working with a legend like Norman Petty, that experience didn't shape my life or career nearly as profoundly as the years I spent in Don Caldwell's original recording studio on Avenue Q in Lubbock. Well-known singer-songwriter-artist, Terry Allen, who recorded many of his critically-acclaimed albums at Caldwell's, dubbed the little studio, "The only mountain In Lubbock."

I recorded vocal and guitar demos of some of my earliest compositions in Don's facility, when he had a little two-track recording machine, empty egg cartons on the wall to dampen the echoes, and no carpet on the floor. During my first recording session there, Don kept interrupting and reminding me not to tap my foot, as the sound bled into the vocal mic and sounded like a loose boot in a worn-out clothes dryer.

Don soon upgraded to a four-track machine, then was graciously loaned an eight-track machine by Leon Russell's Shelter Records studio in Tulsa, Oklahoma. Later, the studio added a somewhat cantankerous sixteen-track machine that sometimes required someone to hold their finger on the take-up reel to insure the speed remained constant. This was back in the day of analog tape recording, with big two-inch recording reels. The individual tracks were mixed down to a stereo ¼-inch tape machine that would be sent to a record pressing plant and converted into 45 rpm singles, LP albums, cassettes, or 8-track tapes. Tape editing "cut and paste" was literally done with a utility knife and ¼-inch splicing tape.

Under the tutelage of Lloyd Maines, I learned the art of being a studio musician. Working with Lloyd in the studio was a humbling experience, but made me a much better musician than I thought I could ever be. No matter what amount of natural talent and skill a musician, songwriter, or artist has, Lloyd has a knack of squeezing-out and magically capturing every ounce of it. I learned how to really listen in the studio, perfected my arranging and charting skills, and discovered that less is generally better. I also learned that the answer is always yes. The first time I ever picked up a mandolin was to play on a song in the studio, and the first time I ever played an accordion was on a Terry Allen recording. Those who have had the honor of working with Lloyd understand the humor and profound professionalism and commitment to excellence he brings to the recording process. In his own words, his Grammy-winning record production philosophy is to make a record "in tune, in time, and under-budget."

| TORTURED |

In the mid 1980's German filmmaker, Wolf-Eckart Buhler, produced a documentary entitled Amerasia. Terry Allen was hired to write, produce, and perform the musical sound track for the movie. The recording was an interesting mix of Terry's original music performed and recorded in Thailand with Thai musicians, and at Don Caldwell studios in Lubbock with the Panhandle Mystery Band. One particular song is called The Burden. At the end of the tune, Terry asked me to play a "60's sounding, psychedelic, hard rock, Viet Nam jungle, Jimi Hendrix style electric guitar solo." After listening to the track several times in the control room, I took my 1976 Gibson Les Paul into the recording booth, plugged it into a Marshall amplifier, turned it up to 11, and played the wildest solo I could possibly play. I honestly didn't think it was very good, and felt like I could play it much better with a few more takes. Terry loved it and insisted we use it for the soundtrack. I was happy that he was happy, but still thought I could have played it better. Terry told me he felt I had transcended myself. I guess my transcendence had captured the passion of the moment, and Terry didn't want to change a single note.

Several years later, Vintage Guitar Magazine had a feature article on Terry Allen and the Amerasia soundtrack. The article mentioned my solo on The Burden song, referring to it as "tortured." I took that as high praise.

That little recording studio on Avenue Q was a sanctuary of creativity for musicians, songwriters, artists, and bands from literally all over the world. It was a place overflowing with music, art, good ideas, bad ideas, new ideas, hit songs, crappy songs, great playing, soulful singing, professionals, amateurs, legends, has-been's and wannabes. It was a holy shrine brimming with daily doses of truth, wisdom, tall tales, and good old-fashioned West Texas B.S. It was an ashram littered with coffee-stained song lyrics and chord charts; empty beer cans and fast food boxes; whiskey bottles, overflowing ashtrays, and the occasional giant cockroach. We held it in great reverence. All of us who wrote, recorded, arranged, produced, and engineered learned not only the art of studio production, but the essential elements of the music business. Whether it was recording a gospel music session, a thirty-second commercial jingle, a movie sound track, a full-blown album, or a simple publisher demo-track, we learned how to manage time, how to arrange on the fly, how to cooperate and be patient with temperamental artists and clients, how to take direction from producers and engineers, and how to be tolerant and respectful of others' opinions and ideas. (Not always an easy or pleasant task).

Be it the gospel recordings of Johnny Ray Watson and Jim Fullingim, the folk music of Andy Wilkinson, the new wave rock of The Nelsons, the Texas country and Americana of Terry Allen, Joe Ely, The Maines Brothers Band, Pat Green, legendary songwriters Sonny Curtis and J. D. Souther, or any of the myriad other great artists, the music that came out of Don Caldwell studios has given the world a soulful, loving, lasting and living legacy.

> *It was a place overflowing with music, art, good ideas, bad ideas, new ideas, hit songs, crappy songs, great playing, soulful singing, professionals, amateurs, legends, has-been's and wannabes.*

THE SONGS: PART II

All of us who grew up in the '50's and '60's understood the joy of going down to the local five-and-dime store to purchase the latest 45 RPM single of our favorite band. Those little round discs with the large holes in the center had the Big Hit song from the artist on one side and a "throw away song" on the flip side. Every so often an artist would have a 45 with hits on both the A and B sides, and sometimes the B side would actually be a pretty cool song. If you had the right kind of record player, with the right kind of spindle attachments, you could stack several of your favorite records, and the player would play them in succession, sort of a precursor to today's digital playlists. For the B side songwriters, there was no fame or artistic recognition, but you received the same royalty payments for records sold as the writer of the hit, so you could say you had a cut and were indeed a professional songwriter.

Over the course of my songwriting career I experienced so many disappointments, rejections, failures, heartaches, and broken promises that sometimes it seemed useless to continue. What was the point of writing if no big star would record my songs? I began to feel I just wasn't good enough to be a famous professional songwriter. I began thinking of myself as the musical equivalent of Crash Davis, Kevin Costner's character in the film, Bull Durham, always flying just below the radar of career significance. However, something happened along the way that I would never have anticipated. I realize now that at the times of my deepest despair about my career, God began presenting opportunities for me to write songs that weren't meant to be hits, but provided me the joy of writing, and rekindled my creative fire. I wouldn't realize till much later in life how important these small opportunities would become. Here are a few examples of those fortuitous circumstances.

FELIX THE KOUNTRY KAT

My friend and music business mentor, Bud Andrews, was a radio host at KFYO 790 AM in downtown Lubbock. During the mid-1970's KFYO programmed mostly news, sports, local talk, and easy listening music. The station decided to begin a country music format from midnight to 6 a.m and hired Felix "The Kountry Kat" Franklin as the on-air personality. Bud introduced me to Felix, who was quite a character, and he and I became good friends. I spent many a midnight hour at the station, fascinated by the radio business and the stories he would tell about his wild and crazy younger days. One evening, not long after the show had begun airing, I was sitting in the radio station and got the idea for a thirty-second theme song for his radio show. We recorded it right there, and Felix began playing it every night at the beginning of his show.

> *Every night around midnight, turn on your radio,*
> *Listen to the music, on the all night Country show.*
> *It's Felix the Kat in his cowboy hat, playin' them records till dawn.*
> *Turn on your radio and listen to a country song. Listen to a country song.*
> *Listen................................ to the The Kountry Kat*

The show ran for a few years, and though I was never paid a single cent for use of the song, I was proud that Felix considered my talent worthy of inclusion.

WHO WILL LOVE ME

Carol and I adopted our two children, Katie and Cody, with the tremendous help, generosity, and support of our family, friends, and some very special people involved with adoption-related services at the State of Texas: Jonette Walker, our advocate and attorney, Nannette Peterson, our case worker, and Sherry Fleming, who worked with several child-advocacy agencies in West Texas. Not long after our adoption was finalized, Sherry approached Lloyd Maines about recording a musical jingle for an advertising campaign to promote adoption and foster care services by West Texas Child Protective Services. Given my involvement and firsthand knowledge of the adoption process, I was honored to be asked to write the jingle. They wanted a short thirty-second Public

Service Announcement that would be played on radio, in conjunction with a short video clip for television. Lloyd recorded me with a simple guitar/voice demo and played the song for Sherry and some folks at Child Protective Services. They liked the song, titled Who Will Love Me, but thought it might be more effective if sung by a nine or ten-year-old child. Lloyd said he knew the perfect voice and proceeded to make a simple recording using only guitar and his nine-year-old daughter, Natalie. This may have been one of the first professional recordings of Natalie Maines' career. The commercial jingle was very successful, running for several months on West Texas area radio and TV. A couple of years later, Lloyd's sister, LaTronda Maines Moyers, with Lloyd's daughters, Kim and Natalie, added additional verses to the song, and Latronda included the new version on her solo gospel album, Labor Of Love. So, yes, I have co-written a song with Natalie Maines.

A couple of my co writers for "Who will love me" LaTronda Maines Moyers and Natalie Maines at a West Texas Music Association Jam at Buffalo Springs Lake
Photo courtesy – Alice Smith

Who will love me, who will take care of me?
Does anybody, need somebody like me?
Someone be there, someone please care.
Who Will Love Me?

Who Will Love Me © 1985 Cary C. Banks, additional lyrics by LaTronda Maines Moyers, Kim Maines Maguire, and Natalie Maines

RICE KRISPIES SONG

Fairly early in my songwriting career I wrote a jingle for Rice Krispies cereal. Being a naive, young writer, I figured I could mail a tape of the jingle to the Kellogg's Corporation, they would hear it and love it, use it in a massive advertising campaign, and pay me lots of money. I would later learn that it doesn't work that way. Big corporations hire big advertising agencies, who have teams of jingle writers to create songs for product ads. I imagine my tape went directly into the proverbial round file in the mail room at the Kellogg's corporate headquarters. It was a fun little song I played for my friends. Decades later Ann Powell, my friend from those early days, came to one of my gigs and requested the Rice Krispies song. She remembered all the lyrics, and when I couldn't recall them, she had to school me on my own song. Now that's a true fan.

It's a good, good mornin' getting' up and get around.
It's a good, good morning get your feet on the ground.
It's a good, good feelin' gonna last all day.
It's a good, good mornin', the Kellogg's Rice Krispies way

LOVE WILL LEAD THE WAY

In 1989, Carol and I and our kids were attending Saint John's Methodist Church in Lubbock when the church asked me to be a member of the Administrative Board. What an eye-opening experiment that turned out to be, but that's another story. The church was planning a big 50th Anniversary celebration of its founding and wanted to use a particular Contemporary Christian song as part of the ceremonies. When members of the board inquired about using the song, they were informed by the publisher that it would cost a certain amount for the church to license it. The board members thought the licensing fee outrageous and decided that maybe the celebration would have to do without a special song.

One of the board members, Carol Petersen, spoke up. "We have a professional songwriter on our board," she said, smiling at me. "We should have Cary write a song for us." The board was highly in favor of this, so a few days later I scratched out some lyrics for a verse and chorus, and sang Love Will Lead The Way for the board. They loved it and said they would commence with planning the celebration. I didn't think any more about the tune until a couple of weeks before the event, when a board member asked me how the song was coming along. Realizing I hadn't finished it, I offered a little white lie (right there in the church building) and said the song was ready to go, and I'd have a recording to them within the next couple of days. I finished the song that day, recorded it with one of the congregation's choir members, Ruby Moultrie, and presented it in time for the celebration. Once again, I was never offered any compensation for my services, but I hadn't expected any, and was honored that the church would use my song for such an auspicious occasion. We left the church soon after that, but I understand the congregation still sings the song in worship services from time to time.

There is hope for tomorrow, in the dreams of yesterday,
there is strength for the hard times that face us every day.
We've been blessed with a promise, the good Lord gives each day.
All along our pilgrim journey, Love Will Lead the Way
Love Will Lead the Way, Love Will Lead the Way
All along our pilgrim journey, Love Will Lead the Way
In the eyes of the children, we see our hopes and fears.
We gather faith and wisdom from those who've seen the years.
With a spirit of thanksgiving for God's high and holy grace,
we celebrate our living with a song of love and praise.

Love Will Lead the Way ©1989 Cary C. Banks

BOOT CITY, BOOT CITY TOO

In the summer of 1991, local musician, producer and entrepreneur, Don Caldwell, was part of the city of Lubbock's planning committee for a giant Fourth of July celebration, including a parade and a big, nighttime concert with fireworks, featuring local musicians and the civic orchestra. The folks at Civic Lubbock were enthusiastic about the project, but unsure how to finance such a mammoth undertaking. One of the many things Don did to make the event successful was to approach local businesses to underwrite the cost. One such business was Boot City, a successful western clothing store. They had recently opened a second location, and eager to promote both stores, told Don they would help underwrite the event if he would produce an advertising jingle for their business. A few days later Don and I sat down at his recording studio and recorded thirty seconds of my playing a folky/country fingerpicking guitar part while Don hummed a bluesy melody, ending with a vocal stinger "Boot City, Boot City Too." Recording Engineer, Mark Murray, added a light percussion part, and the folks at Boot City loved it. The Fourth On Broadway celebration was a huge success and has grown into the largest annual one-day community celebration event in the country. Boot City has continued to use that same jingle for over twenty-five years.

Over the years I wrote several other commercial jingles, including songs for Jack and Jill Donuts, Chick 'n Sea restaurant, The Depot restaurant, (now home to the Buddy Holly Center) Jack T's Music World, Edward's Electronics, and Western Bank Artesia. I wrote That's How You Grow A Great Kid for Covenant Children's Hospital, and several "spec" (speculation) jingles that never made it past the demo stage. I can tell you, truly, that writing a good and effective thirty-second jingle is as challenging as writing a good and effective three-minute song. My friends, Jay Lemon and Junior Vasquez, have become masters of the thirty-second jingle, and I am in awe of their wit, talent, and prolific production output.

| PARODIES, PLAYS AND PROJECTS |

The more I embraced songwriting as an art, a skill, a calling, and a gift from God, the less I despaired about not having a Number One record, or winning a Grammy, or even being recognized for my talents or achievements. For more than forty years I have been blessed with opportunities to write commercials, theme songs, a country/gospel stage musical, Wild Heart, with Jay Lemon, a performance-art collaboration project, Stories From The Storm Cellar, with my friend, Paul Milosevich, songs for friends, songs for my grandkids, songs for special occasions, and even musical parodies. My favorite parody was for my friend, Judy Shema, when she was ordained as a minister in the Methodist Church. I wrote She's No Lady, She's the Preacher, a parody of Lyle Lovett's She's No Lady, She's My Wife.

I had the exquisite joy of collaborating on an original song with my daughter, Katherine Jean Banks. While attending Texas Tech, she took a course in creativity from my friend, Andy Wilkinson. Part of the requirements were that she compose an original song to go with an art project she was creating. The lyrics to Katie's song, Surviving The Storm, were essentially a fictionalized version of the story of her great-grandmother, Nancy Pettigrew Grantham, and the struggles she faced growing up in the wilds of Eastern New Mexico, enduring two world wars, the infamous Dust Bowl storms, and the Great Depression. I added the melody to Katie's words and recorded a simple demo in the Waylon Jennings Studio at South Plains College. Katie got an A in the class.

One of the most fun moments of my entire career was co-writing a song called Hiney Bone with my son, Cody, and my grandson, Jaxon.

One evening, Cody told a bedtime story about a crazy clown to then five-year-old Jaxon. Sometime later, Jaxon told his version of the story to his mom, Tiffany, who recorded it on her iPhone and sent the recording to me. I put the story in song form and recorded it with fellow instructors at the Waylon Jennings Studio. Some creative students in the Design Communications Department at South Plains College produced a cute, animated video of the Hiney Bone song that can be seen on YouTube.

Once there was a circus clown who thought that he was funny.
He climbed up on a tightrope wire and started actin' like a dummy.
He started jumpin' up and down, jugglin juggle balls all around,
but when he slipped and he fell down, he yelled out as he hit the ground
Hiney Bone, Hiney Bone I think I broke my Hiney Bone.
It hurts real bad, I feel so sad, I think I broke my Hiney Bone
His friends took him to the hospital and the Hospitaler said,
"We have to take your temperature and put you in the bed."
The doctor came and looked at him and said "Well, it could be worse,
but you didn't break your Hiney Bone, your Hiney Bone just hurts."
Hiney Bone , Hiney Bone I think I broke my Hiney Bone.
It hurts real bad, but the doctor said, I didn't break my Hiney Bone.

Hiney Bone © 2013 Cary C. Banks, Cody Banks, Jaxon Banks

I suppose in the world of Top 40 charts, Platinum-selling recordings, and Song of the Year awards, some might consider my "almost like a professional" songwriting career just a series of B sides. That may be a fair assessment, and I may never be included in the company of songwriting greats Jimmy Webb, Merle Haggard, or John Mayer. However, I have written some pretty good songs and have, over the years, found a loyal and faithful audience. It seems the less seriously I began to take my songwriting failures, the more seriously people began to take my songwriting.

THE ARTISTS

As a songwriter, I have been blessed to have my songs recorded by some very talented singers. Here is a list (to the best of my recollection) of the wonderful and gracious artists who have recorded my songs. I have recordings of almost all these, some dating back to the days of LPs, 45 rpm singles, 8-track tapes, cassettes, and on to the world of compact discs, downloads, and internet streaming.

Maines Brothers Band- Ain't Nobody Lonely, Love is a Gamble, Easy to Love, You are a Miracle, Panhandle Serenade, Let the Rain Come Down, Gonna be a Cowboy

Jerry Brownlow- More Love

Jerry Jordan- I Can't Sing A Love Song

Free Whiskey- Gonna be a Cowboy, Fools Like Me, I Like You, Makin' Love, Heart Breakin' Woman, Ain't Nobody Lonely

Jack Tyson- Fools Like Me, Turn Off the Tv, Till Love Comes Again, Angel in My Arms

Johnny James- Ain't Nobody Lonely, Albuquerque Callin', Why I Love the Lady, Will You Remember Me Then, You Hurt Me, Cheatin' Night, Gonna Be A Cowboy, I Just Couldn't Back The Tears, Something Changed

Liz Lawson- Here I Am on the Radio

Floyd Brown- Fools Like Me

Jim Fulingim- Sing a Song for Jesus

Jeremy Crady- A Country Boy Lost

Cheyenne Ward- Make Some Noise, I'll take My Chances with Love

Floyd Mitchell- Turn Off the TV, Love is a Gamble

Buddi Day- Lovin' Time of Night

Earline Collins- Easy to Love

Willie Redden- Albuquerque Callin'

Larry Hale- Fools Like Me

Scott Meeks- Easy to Love

Lynn Broadus- Fools Like Me

Erroll Mahal- Love is a Gamble

Shawna Cope- Darlin' Let's Do It Again

Billy Langwell- Darlin' Let's Do It Again
Larry Johnson- Lifetime Guarantee

MACARTHUR PARK

I was aware that a young songwriter from Oklahoma had written Glen Campbell's By the Time I Get to Phoenix and the Fifth Dimension's Up Up and Away, but it wasn't until the summer of 1968 that I began my journey as a lifelong fan and avid devotee of Jimmy Webb. The first time I heard the plaintive voice of the wild Irish actor, Richard Harris, cascading out of the AM radio in my '65 Corvair, I felt as though I had entered an alternate universe. It was the same feeling I had seeing the Beatles on the Ed Sullivan Show. The song was over seven minutes long and had several different sections, including an instrumental section that was a genius combination of classical and rock, and a glorious ending with a soprano voice hitting a high B flat. The critical and chart-topping success of MacArthur Park signaled that all the rules had changed, all bets were off, and all things were possible. A long-haired beauty who I had an enormous crush on graciously lent me her copy of the Richard Harris A Tramp Shining album that featured MacArthur Park, and I literally wore it out before she sweetly but firmly requested I give it back and go buy my own. I bought my own album and a Jimmy Webb songbook; and my former bandmate David Crawford, an incredibly talented musician and piano player, showed me the basic chord progression of the middle instrumental section of the song. My friend and gifted tenor, Danny Johnson, from my original band, and I worked up an arrangement of the song and performed at banquets, parties, and various soirees. After one of the shows, a nice lady who was a piano teacher, approached me and gently reprimanded

> *The critical and chart-topping success of MacArthur Park signaled that all the rules had changed, all bets were off, and all things were possible.*

my piano technique. "You have to lay off that sustain pedal, young man," she suggested. "It makes everything you play sound mushy and cluttered." It was a truthful critique of my lack of good technique, and a lesson that I would, years later, share with my own piano students. I credit MacArthur Park as the single-most influential song that inspired me to want to be a professional songwriter. Forty years later I would have the honor of meeting Jimmy Webb at a small venue in Oklahoma City called The Blue Door. In 2009, I recorded a guitar instrumental version of MacArthur Park and other Jimmy Webb songs on my CD, Guitar Out in the Rain. I was honored to have my name listed in Jimmy's book, "The Cake and the Rain," among the artists who have recorded the song.

For a time during the 1980's I was a member of the Administrative Board at Saint John's United Methodist Church in Lubbock. On the occasion of one particular board meeting, various members of the committee had arrived a little early and were engaged in light conversation. One of them was a gentleman named Johnny Poff, who was in the radio broadcasting business, and he and I had developed a friendship as our paths sometimes crossed in the workplace. As I recall, Johnny and I were engaged in some light conversation about the music and radio business, when the subject oddly drifted into songs we considered stupid. Johnny, who had been in the business a long time, professed that he thought the worst song ever recorded was that stupid tune about the cake melting in the rain: MacArthur Park. Various other members joined the discussion and began voicing their opinions about songs they thought stupid or inane. Everyone was having a good laugh as various tunes were mentioned but I—a bit annoyed at Johnny's comment—just smiled and held my peace.

As was his way, our gracious and gentle pastor, Ted Dotts, shifted the topic to a story of one of his former parishioners who was suffering a terminal illness. Ted said the old gentleman had called him to his bedside shortly before his death to discuss funeral arrangements. Ted inquired what specific things the old man wanted said or done at the funeral. He took Ted's hand and said, "Pastor, if you just make sure that When We All Get to Heaven is sung at the beginning of the service, the rest of the funeral will take care of itself." The story was very moving and prompted a discussion about what special song each of us might want sung at our own funeral. Amazing Grace, How Great Thou Art, Farther Along, and other classic hymns were mentioned one by one as all the board members except me named their specific song. After a brief and awkward silence, Pastor Ted looked at me and asked, "So what would our resident musician like sung at his funeral?" I smiled and looked directly at Johnny Poff and proudly proclaimed: MacArthur Park.

It took several minutes for the meeting to come to order as Johnny could not stop laughing.

THE WEST TEXAS MUSIC HOUR IS ON THE AIR

In the spring of 1987, Lloyd Maines approached me with the idea of our hosting a radio show exclusively featuring West Texas artists, musicians, and songwriters. I thought it was a great idea, but wondered how much it would cost us to buy an hour of time at the most successful radio station in town: KLLL 96.3 FM. Lloyd arranged a meeting with Scott Harris (aka John Steele) and the management at KLLL, told them our idea, and asked what they would charge us to do the show. They asked Lloyd what time slot he was considering, and he said 8:00-9:00 p.m. on Sunday Night. (We would later change that time to 9:00-10:00). They told Lloyd that wasn't a profitable slot for the radio station, as no advertisers would buy time on Sunday night, and if we really wanted it, we could have it for free. We found out later the management thought it amusing that some musicians wanted to do a radio show. They assumed we would quickly run out of material to play and get tired of trying to find advertisers at such a unprofitable hour. They gave us about six weeks before we abandoned the project.

Nevertheless, the first Sunday night in March of 1987, the West Texas Music Hour launched its first broadcast. One of our goals was to feature both

We found out later the management thought it amusing that some musicians wanted to do a radio show.

new and long-established West Texas talent, and as a signature aspect of the show, play at least one Bob Wills' and one Buddy Holly song every episode. During the years that we did the program, we greatly expanded the geographical reaches of West Texas, but always kept the soul of the show tied to its West Texas roots.

The broadcast originally featured Lloyd and Kenny Maines, Richard Bowden, and myself as co-hosts. Not long after it began, Richard relocated to Austin; and for the rest of our tenure it was the remaining three of us, along with an occasional guest host. We always started the show with The Maines Brothers Band instrumental, Farm Road 40, a tune Lloyd had written, and our signature phrase: "The West Texas Music Hour is On the Air." Womble Oldsmobile and Kyle's 88 Key Café were among the first advertisers, and the commercials were all live, unrehearsed sales pitches from Lloyd, Kenny, and me. We later added some faithful and supportive sponsors such as Moyers Sound Studio and Caprock Café. The show was loose and fun, and soon developed a fairly large and loyal local audience. Of all the great times we had doing the broadcast, the most enjoyable were when artists dropped by the studio to perform live. We would often squeeze guitarists, fiddlers, singers, even percussionists into the small control room, bunch them around two Sennheiser Broadcast microphones, and let 'er rip. We taped many of the sessions, and the quality of the live performances was amazingly good and well-balanced. For several years, our good friend, Charles Chambers, recorded almost every show we broadcast.

We would often squeeze guitarists, fiddlers, singers, even percussionists into the small control room, bunch them around two Sennheiser Broadcast microphones, and let 'er rip.

Just a few of the notable artists that graced our program over the years included, Joe Ely, Butch Hancock, Jimmie Dale Gilmore, Kimmie Rhodes, Jesse Taylor, Robert Earl Keen, Ramblin' Jack Elliot, Sonny

Throckmorton, Sonny Curtis, Terry Allen, Willis Alan Ramsey, Heath Wright, Joe Carr and Alan Munde, Tommy Anderson, Doug Smith, Donnie Allison and John Sprott, Andy Wilkinson; a couple of young up and coming singer/songwriters, Jack Ingram and Pat Green; and a little trio from Dallas called the Dixie Chicks. For our fifth anniversary, we did a two-hour broadcast from Don Caldwell studios, where a host of local musicians and songwriters performed live in the studio.

In eleven years of broadcasting the West Texas Music Hour, we had many memorable moments. A couple of the most unforgettable were:

THE TUMBLEWEED CHRISTMAS TREE

Very early on we began to broadcast a special Christmas show each December featuring live and recorded songs by local talents such as pianist Doug Smith. We got a lot of positive response from a song Kenny had written called In the Children's Eyes, and it inspired me to seek other local songwriters who had original Christmas songs. A few weeks before one of our holiday shows, I asked local songwriter, Andy Wilkinson, if he had any original Christmas songs. He gave a chuckle and said he'd never considered writing one. A short time later, he called and said he and Lloyd were in the process of recording a little Christmas tune he had just written and would bring it by for us to play on the air. The song was titled The Tumbleweed Christmas Tree. It was a cute story about a poor oil-field family in No Trees, Texas discovering a unique way to celebrate Christmas. The song was an instant hit on the show, and a couple of years later Andy performed it live on Christmas morning in No Trees for the NBC Today show. Yes, Virginia, there really is a place called No Trees, Texas.

SHE'S NO LADY, SHE'S MY WIFE

For the first couple of years we would take turns answering the phone on the listener call-in line during the broadcast, and we got some pretty interesting responses to the music we played. One particular night I was on phone duty when a lady, obviously inebriated, called to voice a complaint about a song we had played.

"KLLL, West Texas Music Hour," I answered.

"Hey" she blubbered, "are y'all the one's juss played 'at song, she aint no lady, she's muh wife?"

"Yeah, that was She's No Lady, She's My Wife, by Lyle Lovett. It's a great song, don't you think?"

"Hell, no!" she yelled. "That song's awful. A man aint s'posed to say stuff like 'at 'bout his woman. The Bible says a man's s'posed to love and respect his woman. Tha's a turrble song and y'all oughta be 'shamed of playin it."

She continued to rant and rave for about five minutes. Finally I had to say, "Ma'am, I'm sorry you didn't like the song but we appreciate you listening; I hope you have a nice evening."

She wasn't done with her drunken rant, and before I could politely hang up she said, "I tell you what, if my ole man ever said sumpin' like 'at to me, you know what I'd do?" Before I could even respond to her rhetorical question she added, "Well, I'd kick his ass. That's what I'd do."

Following that little exchange, we stopped answering the phone during the show.

We indeed lasted way past the predicted six weeks and continued broadcasting the West Texas Music Hour for eleven years, until the summer of 1998. We signed off our final broadcast with Robert Earl Keen's The Road Goes on Forever, and the Party Never Ends.

THE VOICE

I've been called a lot of things in my life but a great singer has never been one of them. I've always loved to sing, and from my years singing a capella hymns in the Church Of Christ, I developed a pretty decent ear and a love for harmony. From the time of my earliest groups I never shied away from singing the lead part, but I always knew my voice was less-than-spectacular . . . way less. I always wanted to sing bass, but I discovered in junior high choir I was—and always will be—a tenor. Not a tenor like Vince Gill or Steve Perry, just an ordinary garden-variety tenor with a fairly limited range. Neil Diamond songs were always too low; Robert Plant and Harry Nilsson tunes always too high. I never had any formal vocal training, so my only vocal technique came from singing in honky tonks, where you basically belt it out as loud and as hard as you can for as long as you can.

There came a time when I was singing six nights a week in smoky honky-tonks, smoking two packs of cigarettes a day, and wondering why I kept a persistent cough and sore throat year-round. I finally—and reluctantly—went to see an ear, nose, and throat specialist, who explained I had a severe case of chronic bronchitis. He asked what I did for a living, and I proudly proclaimed I was a singer-song-writer-musician. He asked me if I smoked (as if he couldn't already tell), and I had to confess that I did. He looked me straight in the eye and said, "You're not taking very good care of your instrument, are you?"

It was at that point, after smoking heavily for more than a decade, that it hit me: If I was going to continue having a career, it was time to give up the cigs. It wasn't easy, but I quit cold-turkey and haven't had a single puff since March 2nd, 1981. As the great West Texas musician and philosopher, Tommy Hancock, once opined. "If you want to quit smoking, you have to . . . quit smoking." I believe that one of the saddest ironies of the music business is that two of the greatest popular voices ever recoded, Nat King Cole and Harry Nillson, were both heavy smokers. Nat King Cole died at age 47, and Harry Nillson, at age 53.

While my voice isn't bad, it's not strong, not powerful and resonant, and definitely not radio-friendly. I'd never make it past the first round of a singing competition like American Idol or The Voice. Though early-on in my career I sang my own song demos, I quickly learned that having better singers perform my songs greatly increased my chances of being heard. I have been fortunate to work with great vocalists like Kenny Maines, Jerry Brownlow, Robin Griffin, Jack Tyson, Johnny James,

> *I never had any formal vocal training, so my only vocal technique came from singing in honky tonks, where you basically belt it out as loud and as hard as you can for as long as you can.*

Jason Wyatt, Terri Sue Caldwell, Janalei Potrament Stoval, and others who bring a special richness, beauty, and soul to my songs. Over the years, I've learned to choose humorous and story-telling songs that I can sell, and that people will believe me singing. Many songwriters realize if no other artists are recording your songs, you have to sing them yourself to the best of your ability. Many of my favorite songsmiths aren't great singers by any stretch, but I love the soulful honesty of their recordings.

While I will never be numbered among the great vocalists of popular music like Nat King Cole, Frank Sinatra, Harry Nilsson, Vince Gill, and Paul McCartney, I've learned to embrace my limited abilities and to make the most of my less-than-great vocal instrument. To quote my friend Dr. Jerry Goolsby, "If you can't fix it . . . feature it."

OH LOOK . . . TANYA TUCKER!

In May 1993 I had the extreme honor, as part of The Maines Brothers Band, of being inducted into the West Texas Walk of Fame. At that time, The Walk of Fame and the Buddy Holly Statue were located on Avenue Q, just west of the Civic Center. It has since been moved to the Buddy and Maria Elena Holly Memorial Park at 19TH Street and Texas Avenue, across the street from the Buddy Holly Museum. I remain extremely humbled and honored to have received such a wonderful recognition.

My kids, Katie and Cody, were still in elementary school at the time, and one of their neighborhood friends had a cousin from Louisiana staying with the family for a few days. In the course of getting to know the young girl, who was about the same age as my children, they discovered she was a big country music fan. They came running home with the young lady in tow, telling me they had met this new friend who really liked country music and could we Please! go down to the Walk of Fame and show her that I was a famous country star, too?

"Indeed," I said, and we loaded up the van and drove down to the little plot of land that showcased the Buddy Holly statue. Surrounded by a ring of bronze plaques, it featured the names of artists, musicians, actors, and show business folks who had, at one time or another in their

ABOVE: The Maines Brothers Band at our Induction ceremony for the West Texas Walk of Fame at the original location on Avenue Q in Lubbock Texas
Photo courtesy - Maines Brothers collection

LEFT: The Maines Brothers Plaque at the West Texas Walk of Fame
Photo courtesy - Shonda Crutchfield Photography

lives, called Lubbock and West Texas home. There on the Walk of Fame were the names of such notables as Waylon Jennings and Roy Orbison, The Crickets, Barry Corbin, G. W. Bailey, and a host of others, including the newly-inducted Maines Brothers Band. Katie and Cody were so excited for their new friend to see the plaque that they raced across the street and up to it, shouting, "See! There's The Maines Brothers Band, and there's our dad's name, Cary Banks."

I glanced at the young girl, who was completely disinterested in the Maines Brothers plaque. Instead she was jumping up and down, squealing and pointing to a plaque a few feet from ours. "Oh look . . . Tanya Tucker!"

My fifteen seconds of fame had passed ever so quickly.

part six

A LITTLE OL' COLLEGE
WITH A GREAT BIG SOUND

> "Being a professional musician basically means you wake up every morning looking for a job."
>
> - Lloyd Maines

THE LITTLE OL' COLLEGE WITH THE GREAT BIG SOUND

In January of 1993 my friend, Bonnie McCrae, had been asked to join the faculty of the Creative Arts Department at South Plains College in the small West Texas farming and oilfield community of Levelland, Texas. When it appeared there was a need for another piano and vocal instructor, she called and asked if I was interested in a teaching position at the school. I was. Initially a temporary, one-semester-only job, that teaching position turned into a twenty-three year career that possessed, obsessed, and blessed my entire life in so many ways.

The world-renowned Creative Arts Department at South Plains College was the brain child of the school's Dean of Students, Nathan Tubb. Nathan, a distant relative of country superstar, Ernest Tubb, originally envisioned offering guitar classes for college credit for SPC students. When a surprising number of students enrolled in the classes, Nathan saw the potential of an actual community college degree program where students could study all aspects of the commercial music art form, including country & western and bluegrass.

In 1975, Dean Tubb began a nationwide search for someone to head up this new program, and as fate would have it, that led to a professional guitarist and music instrument salesman from Nebraska named John Henry Hartin. Giving up a lucrative job at Conn Music, John accepted the position that would later be titled Chairman of the Creative Arts department, moving his young family to Texas and beginning the mammoth task of creating a curriculum for a brand new, heretofore untried area of music study. Together he and Dean Tubb began the daunting and daring adventure of attempting to attract a new crop of music students to this new program in a little ol' college in the middle of nowhere.

John Hartin is truly one of those quintessential larger-than-life char-

South Plains College Thursday Nite Live Fall 1999 ensemble Bo Carter, Charlie Rapier, Amanda Brown, Lex Reeves, Leslie White, James Randorff, Jason Sever, Lance Smith, Cary C Banks (director), Julie Beaver, Whitney Phipps performing a live television broadcast on the Tom T Hall Stage. Sound engineer, Tim Schoenhals. Photo courtesy - Greg Kreller & Texas Music Office

acters. To understand the tremendous impact he had on South Plains College, commercial music education, and the lives and careers of many students and their families would take an entire book in itself. A veteran of the U.S. Navy, he has traveled on the road playing guitar with Nashville artists Justin Tubb, Redd Stewart, and countless others. A born salesman, he has owned two separate music instrument stores, created Texas Music and Video (one of the world's first successful video music teaching companies), owned and promoted the "E Z Chord" guitar device, and has been known to do whatever it takes to sell his wares. He once donned a giant hat and paraded up and down the walkways at a NAMM Convention, hawking his most recent product. With a wry smile, he loves to relate how he once sold an electronic organ to a family who he later discovered had no electricity in their home. John is also the only musician I know who has been inducted into both the Nebraska Rock & Roll Hall of Fame and the West Texas Walk of Fame.

The Commercial Music program at South Plains College began with a handful of majors who enrolled in private lesson and ensemble classes, music theory and songwriting courses, and other related studies. The program quickly grew, drawing students from literally all over the globe. News of this revolutionary new program caught the attention of well-known songwriter, Tom T. Hall, who was in the process of producing a documentary on bluegrass music, and who eventually traveled to West Texas to view it first-hand. He included the South Plains College students in his documentary, and became very involved and supportive of the program, later establishing the Tom T. and Dixie Hall Scholarship Fund.

In 1980 the school built a state-of-the-art 16-track recording studio and added a Sound Technology degree headed by former student, Randy Ellis. Soon after, a young man named Buddy Jennings from Littlefield, Texas enrolled as a Sound Technology student. Buddy's father, Waylon Jennings, took a keen interest in this budding new program, and in 1982, he and wife, Jessie Colter, donated a Kawai Grand piano to the

World Record Bluegrass Band at South Plains College ...... photo by T.G. Caraway

The World's Largest Bluegrass Band, filling up The Tom T Hall Recording Studio, 1987
Photo courtesy - T G Caraway Collection/Southwest/Collection/Special Collections Library/
Texas Tech University/Lubbock, Texas

recording studio and held a benefit concert on behalf of the program, resulting in the studio being named in Wayland Jennings' honor.

In 1987 the school built a new recording/video studio, adding a video production curriculum entitled Performing Arts Technology. Once again, the old storyteller himself, Tom T. Hall, traveled to West Texas to inaugurate the new facility, which was duly named the Tom T. Hall Recording Studio. Part of the festivities for this new building included assembling over two hundred musicians in the studio to perform as The World's Largest Bluegrass Band. Led by Mr. Hall, this one-of-a-kind band was filmed by instructor Pat McCutchin and the students of the new program, as they performed Fox on the Run, Amazing Grace, and Foggy Mountain Breakdown. Among the pickers in this giant bluegrass orchestra were The Maines Brothers Band, who along with Tom T. Hall, performed a concert that evening.

THAT'S WHY THEY'RE HERE

In the early stages of the program, John Hartin hired well-known, young West Texas musician, Tim McCasland, and Blacksburg, Virginia native, Ed Marsh, to be part of his faculty. This new music education program being one of the first of its kind anywhere, these talented young musicians were given the daunting task of imparting commercial music skills to students of varying degrees of talent and experience. Tim McCasland would often opine that the Fine Arts music programs had centuries of classical composers on which to build their pedagogy curriculum. "They have Bach and Beethoven. We have Roy Acuff and Bo Diddley."

Tim, Ed, and John were daily inventing new and creative ways to teach and train their students in the art and skill of Pickin'. Out in the hinterlands of West Texas, you don't play an instrument, you pick it. You pick the guitar, you pick the banjo, you pick the piano. You do, however, saw the fiddle, whop the drums, thump the bass, and in some cases, holler the vocals. Often the ensemble classes would consist of naturally-gifted students such as fiddler Stuart Duncan—who would become one of Nashville's most sought-after studio musicians—alongside young,

Portrait of John Henry Hartin by Paul Milosevich in the Creative Arts building at South Plains College
Photo courtesy - Chris Hudgins

wannabe musicians with little or no experience or talent. The challenge for these brave instructors was to take this little band of musicians, and somehow put together a set of songs the group could perform at the end of the semester as part of a school mini-music fest. In addition, there were many times John, Tim, and Ed would load up the school van and take their young charges all over the West Texas area to perform for various civic organizations, school assemblies, nursing homes, goat ropin's and pie suppers. The old joke among the faculty was "If two dogs were pissing on a bush anywhere in the area, John Hartin had an ensemble performing for the event."

The program grew exponentially, and John had to hire more faculty musicians. Shortly after he was hired, one new instructor came to John's office to complain about a particular ensemble he was supposed to teach.

"Mr. Hartin, you've got to get me a new ensemble class," the young man said.

"The semester has already begun. We can't just change teachers or give you different students. What's the problem?"

"These kids just aren't any good. They don't know how to read the song charts I gave them. They don't know how to play the right chords or sing the right parts. They just don't know how to play."

John looked the distraught instructor in the eye, and as only he can do, simply said, "That's why they're here."

Those of us who have had the honor of working with John know, love, and appreciate that his talent and creative vision is surpassed only by his humor, his enormously big heart, and his magnanimous generosity.

Just a few of the students from the early years of the program that have gone on to achieve significant success in the music business include Grammy award-winning fiddler, Stuart Duncan; Country Superstar Lee Ann Womack; Heath Wright, lead singer for Ricochet; Ron Block, noted bluegrass musician and songwriter; Mike Bub, award-winning Bluegrass musician; Ricky Turpin, Texas fiddle sensation with Asleep at the Wheel; Edward Perez, Grammy award-winning Latin Music producer; and the late Chris Austin, multi-instrumentalist of the Reba McIntire band.

FASTER THAN I CAN LISTEN

As the bluegrass program at South Plains College gained more success and notoriety, John managed to hire two of the most respected and iconic bluegrass musicians and performers in the world: Legendary banjo player, Alan Munde, and well-known fiddler and multi-instrumentalist, Joe Carr. Joe and Alan had been members of the highly-popular group, Country Gazette, and having them both as part of the faculty instantly put South Plains College on the worldwide musical map. From Australia, Japan, France, England, Scotland, Canada, Israel, South Korea, Venezuela, and other countries, bluegrass enthusiasts of all ages began finding their way to a little community college in Levelland, Texas. Some of the students had grown up listening to the music of Joe and Alan, and were thrilled to come to the Land of the Free and the Home of the Brave to sit at their feet. Some older students would even take sabbaticals from their jobs to come to America for a semester or two to immerse themselves in this original American art form. Retired folks would drive their mobile homes down to Texas and park them for a semester or two. Bluegrass ensemble classes would often showcase an eclectic mixture of young and old, experienced players right next to rank beginners. One particular old-timer was having a hard time keeping up with his younger and more adept classmates. When I asked him how his classes were going, he just shook his head and said, "Man, these young kids can play faster than I can listen."

> *When I asked him how his classes were going, he just shook his head and said, "Man, these young kids can play faster than I can listen."*

At the end of each semester, all the different ensemble classes would perform a thirty-minute set, filmed before a live studio audience in the Tom T. Hall Production Studio. The shows were always family-friendly, open to the public, and absolutely free of charge. We were proud of our facilities, proud of our students, and always wanting them to get real-world performance experience before a live audience. The free shows were also our way of saying thanks and giving a gift back to the hard-working folks of the area, whose tax dollars helped provide the state-of-the-art equipment and facilities we enjoyed.

One particular performance, a crusty older gentleman approached Alan Munde to complain about the students' performances: they weren't as good as last year and didn't play the songs he liked; the temperature in the room was too hot, he expected better—and so on and so on. Finally, the good-natured and ever-patient Alan facetiously asked the gentlemen, "Well, was it free enough for you?"

Joe and Alan, along with Joe's wife, Paula, started a weeklong summer camp at South Plains College called Camp Bluegrass. The event, featuring some of the worlds most well-known and talented bluegrass musicians, draws bluegrass enthusiasts from all over the country. Having run for more than twenty-five years, it is one of the most popular bluegrass events in the nation. Though we lost one of its beloved creators, Joe Carr, in 2015, his indomitable spirit still inspires all those who knew him and were blessed by his music.

MY MAMA SAYS I SANG THEM FAST SONGS PURTY GOOD

During my first semester as an instructor at South Plains College, I had a timid young man enroll in a voice lesson with me. He was actually a welding major, and on the first day of class I asked why he had decided to take voice, and what he hoped to gain from it. He looked down at the floor for a second, then raised his head, gave a shy grin and said, "Well, my mama says I sang them fast songs purty good."

From that moment forward, I knew my time at South Plains College was going to be some kind of adventure with nary a dull moment.

From that moment forward, I knew my time at South Plains College was going to be some kind of adventure with nary a dull moment.

It was an interesting twist of fate that I was hired to teach both piano and voice at South Plains College, as I had no formal, classical training in either. However, by another stroke of luck and good fortune, we hired Mickie Vasquez to teach voice. Like all of us in the Commercial Music Voice program, she had no formal training, but on her own, she researched vocal techniques and made contacts with voice teachers in the Seth Riggs Speech Level Singing Organization. Through Mickie's hard work, combined with the efforts of fellow vocal faculty members Lesa Gailey Thames and Jay Lemon, we established working relationships with Professional Vocal Instructors Dave Stroud, John Henny, Greg Enriquez, and others. Through these relationships, we were able to study the science and art of singing, and South Plains College became one of the first academic institutions to embrace Speech Level Singing, and Mix Singing techniques, thus becoming affiliated with such prestigious organizations as Vocalize U.

WELCOME TO THE SHOW

Not long after I had begun teaching at South Plains College, John Hartin called me into his office. I had only been with the school a couple of years and wondered if I was about to get my walkin' papers. As John was wont to do, he had me sit down, looked directly in my eyes, and said, "I'm going to ask you to do something for me and I want you to say yes." John had a way of getting you to say yes before you even heard the proposal. He told me he wanted to start a school production to showcase the best of our student musical talent, incorporating sound and video students as well, a musical variety show to be filmed in front of a live audience in the Tom T. Hall Production Studio, and broadcast over the South Plains College campus TV station.

"What do you want to call the show?" he asked me. I hadn't even agreed to do the project, and he already expected me to give it a name. That's how John got things done. We agreed the best time to air it was on a Thursday night, so I said, "How about Thursday Nite Live," thinking if we altered the spelling of Night, we might not catch any heat from NBC's Saturday Night Live. We agreed on the name and format, and began the process of auditioning student performers for the ensemble class that would produce and perform the shows. I solicited one of the students in the class, Ron Snow, to help me write a theme song. It wasn't meant to be any great work of art, just a catchy little tune to introduce the show:

> *It's time to gather 'round, for the hottest show in town*
> *When you hear that beat you'll be jumpin' to your feet*
> *It's country, its rock and roll, its R&B. It's Thursday Nite Live at SPC*
> *Welcome to the Show, Welcome to the Show*

© 1995 Cary C. Banks & Ron Snow

Some of the students thought it was incredibly corny, but eventually started having fun with it. The program was broadcast live the first Thursday of every month and re-broadcast on public access channels in the West Texas area on Saturday nights. The song was used at the beginning of every Thursday Nite Live from 1995-2010. Since the song was written in the course of my employment at South Plains College, it is owned by the school, and neither Ron nor I ever received any compensation for authoring it; but it's a great example of creating a work and finding an audience. I loved working with the many students of the various Thursday Nite Live ensembles, and have been honored to see many of them become successful in the music industry.

THAT'S THE ONES WE LIKE

My son, Cody, has been a professional drummer for several years in the Texas Country/Red Dirt music scene. He's performed and recorded with such well-known artists as Stoney Larue, Honey Browne, Djanjo Walker, Brandon Rhyder, Dub Miller, Ryan James, Bonnie Bishop, Kyle Park and many others. When he was in his early teens, he continually begged me to buy him a set of drums. I finally told him if he would join his junior high band, learn to read music, and learn at least the first thirteen essential drum rudiments, I would consider purchasing him a set.

> *I finally told him if he would join his junior high band, learn to read music, and learn at least the first thirteen essential drum rudiments, I would consider purchasing him a set.*

Within one semester, he was first chair snare drum in his band class, was reading complicated sixteenth note rhythms, and could play virtually all the rudiments at an impressive tempo. True to my word, I took him down to a music store owned by my friend, Wally Moyers. Wally gave me a decent price on a used, worn-out set of Pearl drums and even threw in a couple of old cymbals. It seemed like only a few weeks later, I came home to find a rock band practicing in Cody's bedroom.

All through junior high and high school, Cody played at church, school jazz bands and drumlines, and with local bands—many that rehearsed at our home. I had made a point of never interjecting my opinions, critiques, or suggestions to any of the bands Cody performed with unless specifically asked. However, one afternoon a group was rehearsing at the house and working on a cover tune of which I was familiar. The guitar players were mangling the chord progression to the point I could no longer abide the musical malfeasance. I meekly stuck my head inside Cody's room and said, "Excuse me, guys. I hate to butt in, but those are the wrong chords on that song." To which one of the guitar players replied, "Yeah, but that's the ones we like." I just smiled and thought to myself, "How you gonna argue with that?" I decided at that point to turn in my badge and resign from the chord police.

That band, the Thrift Store Cowboys, with lead singer, Daniel Fluitt; brothers Clint and Colt Miller; Kris "Tugboat" Killingsworth; and fiddler and vocalist, Amanda Shires Isbell, would eventually develop a large and loyal regional fan base, and receive critical acclaim for their recordings. Cody, Daniel, Kris, and Amanda were students at South Plains College. Amanda would go on to have a very successful career as an award-winning independent artist with a worldwide following, appearing on the David Letterman Show and also appearing in the Gwyneth Paltrow movie, Country Strong.

LOOKING FOR A DRUMMER

Texas singer-songwriter Bonnie Bishop has been writing songs, making soulful recordings, and traveling the road for several years now, and her song, Not Cause I Wanted To, was recorded by Bonnie Raitt on the Grammy Winning CD, Slipstream. At one point in her career, Bonnie Bishop had employed former South Plains College students, Allison Branch and Jason Newton, in her band. When they left the band, Bonnie began a search for new musicians and planned to attend a show by the Honey Browne Band to check out the drummer, and perhaps persuade him to join her band. She asked her former roommate, Tiffany, to accompany her to the show. Initially, Tiffany showed little interest in going out, but with much persistence, Bonnie finally convinced her to go on this quest to find a drummer.

Tiffany, a stunningly beautiful young woman, made no extra effort to present her most glamourous self that evening, simply donning jeans, a t-shirt, and sandals. She had no intention of meeting or flirting with anyone; she simply went to hang with her friend and enjoy the music. However, during the course of the evening, she became enamored with the drummer of the Honey Browne Band. Bonnie had met the drummer before and introduced him to Tiffany. They seemed to have a real attraction to each other, exchanging phone numbers with the cliché promise that he would call sometime. The very next morning he called to ask if she had plans for the evening. Tiffany told him she was going to hear another band with her mother, Kimberley. Tiffany and the young man had their first date, accompanied by her mom.

The music world turns in many strangely wonderful and unexpected directions, and though Bonnie didn't wind up hiring the young man to join her band, two years later she attended the wedding of her friend, Tiffany Dawn Durham and that drummer, Cody James Earl Banks.

That's the story of how Tiffany became my daughter-in-law and mother of my grandchildren, Jaxon Clay and Paisley Kate Banks.

IT'S LONELY AT THE TOP

PART I - THE UNIVERSITY OF HARD KNOCKS

After a year of being a music major at Lubbock Christian College, I enrolled in the University Of Hard Knocks. It was there I learned the brutal truths and hard facts of both life, and life in the music business. I had a few guitar lessons early on and a couple semesters of piano class in college, but basically I am a self-taught musician. I taught myself to read guitar music and write lead sheets for my songs and those my friends had written. I taught myself how to play the piano and guitar mostly by watching other, better musicians, and listening to the radio and records. Back in the day before internet technology, YouTube videos, and instant access to all things musical, we learned songs by sitting down at the record player, playing the tunes over and over. I wore out many a Beatle's album by moving the needle back again and again to that one guitar lick I was trying to master. When a record began to skip from overuse, we put quarters on the tone arm to give it more weight. When we'd piled four or five quarters and the record still skipped, we knew it was time to buy a new album.

Many people have expressed admiration and a little astonishment at my being a self-taught musician. While it is an admirable quality, it comes with its own set of limitations and hard truths. When you're self-taught, you can only progress as fast and as far as your teacher can lead you. I missed developing a lot of technical skills that would have benefitted me later in my career. But all-in-all I have no regrets. When you enroll in the University of Hard Knocks, your lessons come slower and harder, but they have a much more profound and lasting effect.

> *When you enroll in the University of Hard Knocks, your lessons come slower and harder, but they have a much more profound and lasting effect.*

I learned how to play in a band by listening to what the other members were playing and trying to fit my part to make the whole thing sound better. I learned that democracy doesn't work in a band, that one member has to assume leadership and make the final decisions. I learned that in most cases the other members didn't possess the same drive, ambition, and stick-to-itiveness that I did. I learned that if a band member's girlfriend starts to create trouble in the band, and you confront that member about it, he will always choose the girl over the band. If there is a girl in the band, the guys have to come to terms with the fact that women deal with emotions vastly different than guys. I learned that if you don't daily and relentlessly take care of business, the band will fall apart. I learned that if the band doesn't have a plan and a mission from the get-go, it is destined to break up, no matter what level of success it attains. I also learned some hard emotional life-lessons that substance abuse and addictions will kill a band, no matter how talented the members or close the friendships.

I discovered fairly early in my career that I was probably never going to be a virtuoso guitarist like Chet Atkins or Jose Feliciano, a great a piano player like Leon Russell or Billy Joel, an awesome singer like Harry Nilsson, or a profound and prolific songwriter like Jimmy Webb. Those realizations sparked the idea that if I wanted to survive and have a lasting career in the music business, I had better learn to diversify my talents. Over the years I learned to play the bass, the mandolin, a tiny bit of accordion, and auxiliary percussion instruments; and how to read and write music notation and make myself employable in the industry by discovering as much about it as I could.

Those realizations sparked the idea that if I wanted to survive and have a lasting career in the music business, I had better learn to diversify my talents.

I tried to be as professional as possible, showing up on-time with a good attitude, ready to listen and learn. When you're an independent musician scuffling for gigs, you tend to say yes every time the phone rings, sometimes before you even know who's calling. As Lloyd Maines once famously quoted, "Being a professional musician basically means you wake up every morning looking for a job." Over the years, I also experienced the deafening silence of the phone not ringing. All the ups and downs of my career were pointing me in a direction I would never have imagined until a fortuitous phone call in January 1993 .

I learned a myriad of things about the business: performance, recording, producing, and the art of getting along with fellow musicians and music business folks from my first publisher and producer, Bud Andrews; from producer/engineer/musician; Don Caldwell; from my fellow bandmate, Lloyd Maines; and from my mentor at South Plains College, John Hartin. All these men greatly influenced my life and my career. I consider them great friends and owe each one a debt I can never repay. All the knowledge and skills I acquired about music and the music business in the University of Hard Knocks prepared me most perfectly to be a teacher of Commercial Music in the Creative Arts Department at South Plains College.

| **PART II - FROM HONKY-TONKS TO THE HALLS OF ACADEMIA** |

Not long after helping to create Thursday Nite Live, I was promoted to Program Coordinator of the Commercial Music Program. While this was a giant vote of confidence from my boss and the administration, in reality it was more responsibility, more hours, and more stress for less money. I was awarded tenure, and to his credit John Hartin gave me plenty of latitude and creative control.

My role at South Plains College took on a deeper and more difficult struggle when John retired and the administration named me the new Creative Arts Department Chairperson. At the conclusion of my first week at the helm, driving home late on that Friday—bone-tired, emotionally, physically, and spiritually drained—the thought occurred to me that I had just spent a sixty-hour week as the leader of a world-renowned music school, and had not played one single note of music. That was a harbinger of what was to follow me the next nine years. Along with the new position came the arduous task of shepherding a faculty of artistic and talented musician, sound, and video instructors. I was totally unprepared for the role of leadership of a large department filled with strong-willed, opinionated people, many with their own agendas and ideas of how the department should be run. On top of that was the constant struggle of trying to place the square peg of academia into the round-hole world of rock and roll, blues, and country music, in a time of vastly-changing sound and video technology, all while trying to convince the administration, the Board of Regents, the Texas Education Coordinating Board, and the taxpayers that their funding was being put to good and productive use. I found myself in constant attendance at every advisory board, chairperson, executive council, scholarship committee, curriculum committee, et al. meeting until the word meeting started to sound like a swear word to me. It seemed that almost daily our departmental secretary, Tammy Amos, would bring me a stack of papers, forms, and documents to sign that signified I was assuming responsibility for things, people, and events which were most often completely out of my control. As anyone who has ever been in an administrative position can attest, trying to find and hire qualified and talented people for your organization is extremely frustrating, arduous, and stressful, and having to fire even an incompetent person is even more frustrating, arduous, and stressful.

My career at South Plains College was a series of exhilarating highs, such as being honored by my peers with the Excellence in Teaching Award, or being pictured with SPC student, Julie Beaver, on the cover of the Texas Living section in the June 1999 issue of Southern Living Magazine, to the stingingly painful lows of being publicly belittled and berated by angry parents blaming me for their child being excluded from a high-profile ensemble performance, or being threatened with a lawsuit by a fellow professor. My friend and colleague, Wade McNutt, described my job as "trying to herd a bunch of kittens in a room full of mirror balls." Most of the time, I felt like a glorified traffic cop in a bumper car arena. Despite all the hard lessons learned in the University of Hard Knocks, I soon discovered that no matter what decision I made, someone was going to be pissed off. John Hartin, always prone to add a little levity to any situation, gave me words of wisdom and admonition: "If only 49% of your people are pissed at you at any given time, you're probably doing a pretty good job." He also warned that "If everything seems to be going okay, you probably don't have enough information." While I always appreciated John's humor and encouragement, there were times when it was of little consolation. I fully understood Randy Newman's plaintive tune, It's Lonely at the Top. While I did take heart from the support and encouragement I got from so many of the instructors and staff, I learned some hard les-

Despite all the hard lessons learned in the University of Hard Knocks, I soon discovered that no matter what decision I made, someone was going to be pissed off.

sons about dealing with people. Unlike the apostle Paul, I found that I could not be "all things to all people." I was extremely fortunate that my precious wife, Carol, supported my decision to take the job as Chairperson, and equally supported my decision to step down and eventually retire from the school.

My career as Professor of Music at South Plains College spanned twenty-three years, nine as Chairperson of the Creative Arts Department. During my tenure as Chairman, I had some wonderful experiences and made some lifelong friends. I had the honor of overseeing the construction of a thirteen-thousand square foot addition to our building, and the founding of three additional degrees in Live Sound Technology, Entertainment Business, and Design Communications. I am proud to say our department was able to bring world-renowned professional musicians, songwriters, producers, engineers, and technical people to Levelland for special concerts, seminars, and clinics. Some of these folks would also serve on our advisory boards. Among the incredible talent that graced the Tom T. Hall stage were award winning songwriters Tom T. Hall, Redd Stewart, Richard Leigh, Susan Gibson, Jana Stanfield, Terry McBride, Terri Hendrix, Lloyd Maines, Jeff Hyde, and Clif Magness; guitar greats Doyle Dykes, David Grisham, Clint Strong, Andy Timmons, Johnny Hiland, Joe Bonamasa, Eric Johnson; bluegrass masters Alan Munde, Tony Trischa, Ron Block; jazz saxophonist Brad Leali; bass player Chuck Rainey; piano virtuosos Marcia Ball, Doug Smith, and Anthony Berger; iconic drummers Zoro, Rich Redmond, Stanton Moore, and many others that the students were able to interact with face-to-face, sometimes one-on-one.

MOMENTS TO REMEMBER

I have had many wonderful experiences with the students I was privileged to know and work with at South Plains College. Some of the most memorable moments include the evening I was in my den, about to watch the CMA Awards on TV when the phone rang. It was my former student, Clay Corn, calling from backstage at the show just to tell me he was about to perform with the major artist he was working with at the time. He said, "I just want to thank you for what you taught me and for all the encouragement I received at South Plains College." On a similar note, Scottish guitarist and former student, Craig Smith, called to let me know he was about to perform at the Grand Ole Opry in Nashville, one of several students of mine who have graced the Opry stage. Interestingly, performing on the Grand Ole Opry is a gig I have never had the opportunity to experience myself. Former student, Jason Wyatt, a successful songwriter, artist, and producer in Nashville related to me that he uses every single thing he learned at South Plains College every day in his career. Perhaps the most poignant moment of all was seeing the 2017 CMA Awards tribute to Glen Campbell with Little Big Town singing Wichita Lineman, featuring songwriter Jimmy Webb playing piano, and my Australian student, Jedd Hughes, playing guitar.

ESTEEMED ALUMS

During my time at South Plains College, I had the glorious opportunity to work with some of the most talented young people ever to grace a stage. The following are just some of those students who have achieved notable success in the music and entertainment industry. They include:

Natalie Maines - lead singer/songwriter (Dixie Chicks)

Heath Wright - lead singer and guitarist (Ricochet)

Chad Maines - drummer (Texas Playboys and other Texas acts)

Cody Banks - Noted Texas Drummer (Stoney Larue, Brandon Rhyder, Honeybrowne, Django Walker)

Jedd Hughes - Grammy winning Australian guitarist/songwriter/artist (Rodney Crowell, Keith Urban)

Kym Warner - award-winning Australian mandolin/guitarist/ songwriter/artist (The Greencards)

Jerrod Nieman - hit songwriter/artist, (Lover, Lover, co-author Good Ride Cowboy Garth Brooks)

Richie Brown - hit songwriter (co-author Good Ride Cowboy Garth Brooks)

Jeff Hyde - hit songwriter/musician (Eric Church band, co-author Smoke a Little Smoke Springsteen)

Les Lawless - drummer (Randy Rogers band)

Clare Dunn - artist/songwriter (Universal Music Group Records, Tuxedo, Old Hat)

April Richards Hyde - Operations Manager (Ryman Auditorium, Nashville, Tennessee)

Matt Jenkins - hit songwriter (Cop Car, Song for Another Time, American Beauty, Old Hat)

Jeremy Boreing - Film producer, director, writer, and songwriter (films The Arroyo, Spiral)

Megan Laurie - Australian singer/songwriter (Kissin' the Wind, Light at the End of the Bottle)

Todd Caldwell - Keyboardist (Crosby, Stills and Nash, Kashmir and Burlap; film composer Spiral)

Jason (Kuhn) Wyatt - Singer/songwriter/producer (The Lost Trailers, American Beauty, Sweet Tea Trio)

Jeremy Garrett - Fiddle/mandolin/guitar/songwriter- (Grammy award-winning The Infamous String Dusters)

Jeremy Moyers - Steel guitarist/recording engineer (Lonestar)

Amanda Shires - Award-winning fiddler/songwriter/artist/actress (Country Strong)

Charla Corn - Award-winning vocalist/songwriter/radio personality (Where Have All the Cowboys Gone)

Clay Corn - Keyboardist/songwriter/producer (Pat Green, Stoney Larue, Cory Morrow)

Penny and Katy Clark - bluegrass instrumentalists/vocalist /songwriters (The Purple Hulls)

Ben Clark - bluegrass instrumentalist/songwriter (The Purple Hulls; owner of Banjo Ben.com)

Kyle Aaron (Lopez) - worship leader/multi-instrumentalist (Michael W. Smith, Matt Jenkins)

Craig Smith - Scottish guitar player (Suzy Boggus, Clay Walker, Sunny Sweeney, Jim Lauderdale)

Preston Wait - fiddler/guitarist (Josh Abbott band)

David Fralin - multi-instrumentalist (Josh Abbott band)

Eduardo Salgado - drummer (Josh Abbot band)

Cale Richardson - guitarist/keyboardist (Eli Young Band, Honey Browne Band, Ryan James Band)

Cody Angel - guitarist/steel guitarist (Jason Boland and The Stragglers, School of Rock Instructor)

Erin & Amber Rogers - Grammy-nominated artists/multi-instrumentalists (Scenic Roots)

Waylon Pierce - multi-instrumentalist (Oak Ridge Boys/Neil McCoy)

Jay Saldana – drummer (Williams Clark Green Band, Wade Bowen Band)

Dub Miller - Texas Country singer/songwriter

Jason Newton - drummer (Hogg Maulies)

Steve Harbour - guitarist (Andy Williams PAC, Barbara Fairchild, various Branson Theater shows)

Allie Didriksen Wells - Dove award-nominated children's musical writer (Lillenas Publishing Co.)

Aarun Carter - fiddler/music teacher (Fiddle TV, Mel Bay Publications)

Dustin Garrett - guitarists/singer songwriter/music director (Cactus Theater)

Ryan Garza - singer/songwriter/drummer/producer

Tim Schoenhall - sound engineer/producer/musician (Meaghan Trainor)

Adam Odor - Grammy-winning engineer/producer/musician (The Dixie Chicks)

John Stoll - Director of Audio and Video, (NASA, Houston)

Eric McEnerney - guitarist/vocalist (featured on TV promo ad for the Grand Ole Opry)

Corrina Ripple - fiddler (Flying J Wranglers)

Anne Butts - sound engineer (U2)

Will Boreing - songwriter (film and National commercial muscician with Scott Weiland)

Casey Maines - guitarist (Hogg Maulies)

TEACHING THE TEACHERS

It was also a great delight for me to have guided and trained former students who now teach, or have taught music, sound, or video technology at South Plains College. Those talented folks include:

  Wade McNutt - piano/performance/ensemble instructor

  Allie Huffstutler Maddox - vocalist/vocal instructor

  Matt Quick - instructor/director of the Live Sound Program

  Bethany Borba - vocal/ensemble instructor

  Todd Caldwell - piano/ensemble instructor

  Greg Cook - instructor/video production

  Leslie White Rich - vocal instructor

  Caleb Green - vocal instructor

  Rocky Green - guitar/ensemble instructor

  Zach Nichols - guitar/ensemble instructor

  Michael Garnett - music theory instructor

  Barbara Curry - vocal instructor

  Clay Corn - piano/vocal instructor

  Marcia Hoalting - piano instructor

This little ol' college in the middle of nowhere has truly made an enormous and lasting impact on the music and entertainment world, inspiring countless young musicians, songwriters, sound and video technicians, music teachers, and music business entrepreneurs worldwide.

I can say without hesitation that the faculty and staff of the Creative Arts Department at South Plains College is one of the most intelligent, hardworking, creative, energetic, and fun bunch of people I have ever had the privilege to work with in my life. The department is known and respected worldwide, and the quality of instruction, inspiration, and dedication to excellence is second to none.

part seven

FURTHER ON UP THE ROAD

> "A lot of great inventions were made by someone trying to figure out a way to dodge work."
>
> - Jake Banks

CO-WRITERS

It's been joked in songwriting circles that if you're in the same room when a song is being written, you automatically qualify for a percentage of the writing credits. "Add a word, earn a third," they say. It's been my experience that co-writing is a lot like dating. The first couple of dates may sometimes be a little awkward, but you find out pretty quickly if the relationship is going to work. Although a few of my co-writing experiences have been less than what I had hoped, the vast majority have been enlightening, educational, eventful, engaging , equitable, a lot of fun . . . and sometimes even profitable.

JACK TYSON

Jack was one of those unforgettable characters, larger than life, talented, driven, and prone to excess in everything. When I limped back to Texas after my last Nashville debacle, Jack graciously offered me a job at his music store, Jack T's Music World. Jack was a talented musician with one of the most beautiful baritone voices I'd ever heard. He and I began writing songs together and seemed to have a good creative chemistry. He was in a band named Free Ride, and Johnny and I were in a band called Whiskey Ridge. We decided to combine the two names to form a new group called Free Whiskey. That name caused more than a little consternation with club owners trying to promote and advertise our performances. It seemed the customers were a bit irate on discovering Free Whiskey was the name of the band and not the price of the drink. Some even advertised us as the Free Whiskey Boys to avoid any confusion.

We recorded several of our original songs on an 8-track album, and became very successful in the West Texas area. After winning a Battle of the Bands contest, we started recording original music for a second album financed by Johnny's wife, Annie. One of our songs, Till Love Comes Again, won a quarterfinalist award in the 1978 American Song Festival. Though it was hard playing music till late in the night, then having to get up early the next morning, I stayed committed to my job at the music store and our band.

Unfortunately, with the extracurricular activities and partying lifestyle that Jack embraced, he was neglecting to take care of business at the store. Through a series of unhealthy choices, bad business decisions, and embezzlement of funds by his accountant, he suddenly found himself bankrupt. The store closed and the band broke up shortly thereafter. I discovered how quickly you can go from the penthouse to the outhouse.

In December 2015, the hard-living life of Jackie Winston Tyson finally caught up with him. It was a bittersweet, but most sacred and blessed moment for me to be asked to preside over his funeral service. I was honored to be part of the beautiful celebration of his life, his family, and his music.

| JERRY BROWNLOW |

The first song that Jerry and I collaborated on was You Are a Miracle, recorded by The Maines Brothers Band on the High Rollin' album for Mercury Records. The single made its way into the Top 50's on the Billboard Country charts and the first-round nominations for the Grammy Awards. Jerry and I have a great chemistry together and wrote several other songs that were recorded by The Maines Brothers Band but never released, One particular song, entitled Heart Trouble, was written at my kitchen table. The band did a simple demo of the song and we sent it to our producers at Mercury Records. They liked it, but informed us that Steve Wariner had just released a brand new single called Heart Trouble. It sounded hauntingly similar to the song Jerry and I had written. I guess we had tapped into the same songwriting channel as the Nashville Cats, but Steve got there first. Steve Wariner's record went on to be a Top 10 hit. The song Jerry and I wrote sits somewhere in a box of old cassettes collecting dust in my attic.

One of the favorite songs that Jerry and I co-authored was a tune entitled Dancin' to the Rhythm of Love. As he had done several times before, Jerry brought me a crazy-good chorus. We added a verse and a bridge, and pitched it to The Maines Brothers Band. The band was in the planning stages of our third Mercury Records album. Unfortunately, the album never materialized, and a few months later the band parted ways with Mercury. My friend, Liz Lawson, who had recorded my song, Here I Am On The radio, also recorded her version of Dancin' to the Rhythm of Love, but it was never released. Twenty-five years later, I recorded a version as a duet with the lovely and talented Bethany Borba, for my CD, A Long Time Since It Rained. Just for the record (no pun intended), Jerry and I wrote our song two decades before the Plain White Tees released their giant hit, Sway to the Rhythm of Love. Just sayin'. Jerry has been a close and dear friend for over thirty-five years, and he recently honored me in a most beautiful and profound way by recording my song, More Love, on his album, Using My Bible for a Road Map.

| "WILD HEART" JAY LEMON |

Jay and I were colleagues at South Plains College from 1993 until my retirement in 2015. Jay is an incredibly talented musician, writer, performer, and teacher. Our personalities, music styles, and experiences are 180 degrees opposite. Jay has always been heavily influenced by Funk, R&B, and rock, and I come from a country, gospel, and old-school musical background. While I have always loved and admired Jay's talent, and his humor and quirkiness remains a source of amusement and amazement to me, I would never have guessed he and I would make a successful songwriting team.

Nevertheless, in the fall of 2001, Jay was music worship leader at Trinity Church in Lubbock, and Kevin Rhoads, a minister there, approached Jay with the idea of doing an original country-and-gospel-style musical for the upcoming Christmas season. Our friend and former SPC student, Jeremy Boreing, was working in the film business in California at that time, and Jay talked him into writing the script and directing the play. Jay asked me if I would help him write the songs. While he and

> *I would sit at a little writing table with pen and paper, my guitar on my lap, while Jay would jump up and down on the bed, bouncing a rubber ball off the wall, singing me his ideas.*

I were attending a vocal workshop in Arizona, we set aside some free time to work on the musical. I would characterize our co-writing style as reflecting our respective personalities. I would sit at a little writing table with pen and paper, my guitar on my lap, while Jay would jump up and down on the bed, bouncing a rubber ball off the wall, singing me his ideas. Somehow, we made that work, and within a couple of weeks we had all the songs completed. Thanks to Jay's arranging talent and Jeremy's well-written script, we managed, in a very short time, to assemble a cast of local actors, singers, dancers, and musicians; and produced a professional, original musical called Wild Heart, a moving production that ran successfully for several nights at the church.

CLAY MCINTOSH

Clay McIntosh left a well-paying job as a graphic artist in Oklahoma to come to South Plains College and study songwriting. During Clay's time as a student, he and I developed a personal friendship and songwriting partnership. I helped him put together several songs, and assisted him in learning the art of producing demos in the South Plains College recording studios. Clay's gentle, soft-spoken spirit and generous nature easily earned him the respect and friendship of the younger students, many of whom agreed to play and sing on his demos. Among those featured were Grammy award-winning guitarist and songwriter, Jedd Hughes; hit songwriter and artist, Jerrod Nieman; well-known Texas songwriter and artist, Dub Miller; and the beautiful voices of Janalei Potrament Stoval, Leslie White Rich, Amanda Marie Brown, and Crystal Stanley Wilson. Twenty years later, Clay and I remain good friends and co-writers. Our song, Everyday Hero, is featured on my CD A Long Time Since It Rained. In addition to co-writing, Clay has designed the cover art for all my CD recordings.

| WADE MCNUTT |

I met Wade when he enrolled as a Commercial Music student at South Plains College. Even as a young kid just out of high school, he was already a gifted and accomplished musician and entertainer. He and I developed a friendship. Seeing his potential, I tried to challenge him to broaden his musical horizons, which he did with great intensity, winning student performance awards and demonstrating leadership skills.

After graduation, he toured with Texas Country artist, Doug Moreland, before returning to finish his degree at Wayland Baptist University. A few short years later, I hired him as a piano and ensemble teacher at South Plains College. He quickly became a skilled and successful instructor, and a favorite of the students. I had labored for years to find a piano book and curriculum that would suit the needs of our Commercial Music students, who were required to take a piano course regardless of their major instrument. I had never found anything that I thought would both educate them and let them have fun learning the piano. After much discussion, Wade and I decided to create our own textbook and design our own piano studies curriculum. We co-wrote some songs that explored different styles of commercial music, such as country, rock, R&B, blues, jazz, and gospel. We also arranged some classic piano pieces, transcribed all the arrangements, added some improvisation exercises, and recorded teaching videos for the songs in the book. We called it Play Piano Like a Pro. Wade has included all the videos on his highly successful website, www.pianochops.com and although neither of us are involved with South Plains College anymore, the Commercial Music program still uses the book and videos in the piano studies curriculum. Wade has become successful with not only the pianochops.com website, but also with his pianomediations.com.

Additional talented friends I have had the privilege of co-authoring a tune with include: Lloyd Maines, Mark Paden, Jason Wyatt, Allie Didriksen, Megan Laurie, Rick Vanderpool, Paul Johnson, Randy Christian, Steve Holly, Mike Colclazer, Johnny James, Janet Steely, Thomas C. Jones, Jake Banks and Jim Andrus.

COLLABORATIONS

STORIES FROM THE STORM CELLAR

I was honored to be involved with Stories from the Storm Cellar, the brainchild of artist, Future Akins. The project featured visual and performing artists in a performance art show centered on the West Texas phenomena of sudden and severe weather, showing how the rugged people of the region learned to adapt and survive. I was especially honored to be able to collaborate with legendary artist, Paul Milosevich, for our contribution entitled After the Storm, featuring Paul's beautiful oil painting of a storm passing a golf course, leaving the fairway and green in glistening pools of rainwater. Some of the other artists included: Chester Marston, Steve Teeters, John Chinn, and James Johnson. Songwriters involved in the show included: Donnie Allison, Lloyd Maines,

A collaboration between West Texas artists and musicians
Artwork courtesy - James Johnson

Don Caldwell, Ron Riley, Steve Paxton, Los Tornados, Sara Waters, and Andy Wilkinson. My daughter, Katie, was part of the group that sang the chorus on Andy's song, Things Too Precious for the World.

Story Tellers and Music Makers/ Janis Stalcup

| STORYTELLERS AND MUSIC MAKERS |

Story Tellers and Music Makers was the brainchild of South Plains College Video Production Technology professor, Tom Stalcup, and his producer-friend, Doug Nelson. Filmed in the Tom T. Hall Production Studio, it involved several South Plains College staff and students. The thirty-minute TV show featured Kenny Maines as host (and one episode I hosted), interviewing West Texas songwriters, musicians, producers, and radio personalities. The first season featured thirteen shows which aired on the Texas Tech Public Television Network, earning a nationally-recognized Silver Telly Video Award.

MUSIC FROM LUBBOCK: THE STOCKING PROJECT

In 2009, Westminster Presbyterian Church, in collaboration with students, instructors, and technical professionals from Wayland Baptist University, Lubbock Christian University, and South Plains College, recorded a live-performance CD that was sent to U.S. personnel stationed at Kunsan Air Base in South Korea. Student songwriters from South Plains College, including: Engelo Charles, Alissa Beyer, James W. King, Taylor Hickey, and Dustin Garrett, along with a host of SPC musicians and vocalists, performed original songs for the CD. My performance included my songs, Little One and Ain't Nobody Lonely. Three thousand copies of the CD, along with an assortment of handmade gifts and essential items, were delivered in Christmas stockings to the men and women stationed at the base.

SPC GUITAR COLLECTIVE

Guitar instructors in the Commercial Music Program at South Plains College brought their respective talents together in 2007 to record an album of guitar instrumentals entitled SPC Guitar Collective. The album featured the guitar skills of bluegrass icons, Joe Carr and Alan Munde; the folk/fingerpicking stylings of Mark Wallney and Jerry Stoddard; the rock stylings of Scott Faris and Sonny Borba; the jazz/blues stylings of Brent and Emily Wheeler; the country/pop stylings of Mike Carraway; and the blues stylings of Steve Williams. Steve and I also performed an acoustic medley of gospel songs.

BASEBALL FEVER

Like many young boys growing up in the 1950's, I idolized New York Yankee slugger, Mickie Mantle. My infatuation was so profound that my dad nicknamed me Mick. Living in the middle of West Texas, I never got to see a big league baseball game in person, but I lived for Saturday afternoon and the CBS Game of the Week, with play-by play-announcers Pee Wee Reese and Dizzy Dean. I tried to copy Mickie's swing and his fielding techniques, and kept meticulous records of his statistics. I lived for baseball. I think I was about nine years old when I somehow managed to find the address of the New York Yankees baseball team and sent a letter requesting an autographed picture of my hero. For days and days my friends and I waited anxiously for the mailman to deliver the coveted autographed photo of Mickie Mantle. Glory to God, one day it came. A big envelope from New York City.

I tore in to the envelope, but to my surprise, it was not an autographed picture of Mickie Mantle but a full team photo and other Yankee publicity material. I was instantly disappointed that there was no autographed picture, but was thrilled to have all this stuff from the New York Yankees team. I was the envy of the neighborhood.

I had also sent a separate letter requesting an autographed picture of Yankees' second baseman, Bobby Richardson, another favorite of mine since I had firmly decided I would someday become the Yankees' second baseman. A few days later I received a signed picture and personal letter from him, thanking me for my love of baseball and my interest in him and the team. He continued on in the letter to tell of his belief in, and deep relationship with, Jesus Christ and encouraged me to accept Jesus as my savior. I was not very impressed with that part of the letter, as I was already being dragged to church three times a week and didn't want any more grownups telling me I needed to be saved, even if that grownup was second baseman for the New York Yankees. I didn't realize at the time that he, like all good evangelists, was lovingly planting a seed in my spirit. After he retired from baseball, Bobby Richardson became a minister. Years later, it was a particularly poignant moment for me as I watched Bobby on TV, presiding over Mickie Mantle's funeral services.

I was a pretty decent baseball player and was fortunate to be on the Big Spring Kiwanis Junior League Team that won the Texas State Championship in 1963; but my baseball career never progressed past Junior league after music became my overriding passion. I coached my son Cody's little league baseball teams from t-ball through high school and he was a really good player. My daughter Katie played a season of T-ball but never really enjoyed it that much. "It was too hot," she said. Interestingly, she became an avid baseball fan, learned to keep score on professional score sheets, and collected baseball cards. To this day, any time I visit her, we always try to catch a baseball game.

When my son was playing in the Lubbock Texas Southwestern Little League, I wrote a song called Baseball Fever that I would play for his teammates whenever we had a team party. One of the members of the board at Southwestern Little league asked if we could play a recording of it over the PA system at the ball park. It became a crowd favorite and was played between innings as bumper music for several years at that little league ball park.

> *I remember those long summer afternoon's, sun beatin' down so hot.*
> *Pretending I was Mickie Mantle, on some dusty vacant lot.*
> *I remember those days and the games we played, the dreams we had back then.*
> *When I hear the crack of a baseball bat, I live those dreams again.*
> *It's Baseball Fever, Baseball fever. I catch it every spring.*
> *I love a stolen base and a double play, every pitch and every swing.*
> *I love a 3-2 count with the bases full and a long grand slam home run.*
> *Its Baseball Fever, Baseball fever, keeps me forever young.*

Baseball Fever © 1989 Cary C. Banks

I WANNA BE THAT GUY
STEVE "GITTAR" WILLIAMS

The first time I ever saw Steve Williams was in 1965. He was playing lead guitar with a band called The Blackouts, who were performing for the grand opening of the first shopping mall in my hometown, Big Spring, Texas. I had been playing guitar for about a year, and when I heard this band from Lubbock was coming to town, I was eager to investigate a real rock band up close.

The group specialized in Ventures' music, and Steve's guitar skills just blew me away. He could not have been more than thirteen or fourteen at the time, but he was so good I remember thinking, "I wanna be that guy."

Photo courtesy - Justin Robinett

I did not officially meet Steve until the late 1970s, when Jack Tyson, Johnny James, and I were able to convince him to join the Free Whiskey band.

After Free Whiskey broke up, Steve played with several noteworthy local groups such as Warhorse, but moved to Austin in the late 1980s, where he was lead guitarist for the great piano and blues vocalist, Marcia Ball. When he moved back to Lubbock in the late '90s, we got back together and played in several bands, including The Rex Thomas Band. When he joined the faculty of the Commercial Music Program at South Plains College, we had many performances and recording sessions together with the college's faculty and students.

We have performed as a duo since 2009.

Our first recording as a duo was an instrumental gospel medley featured on the SPC Guitar Collective 2009 CD. My 2010 solo CD, A Long Time Since It Rained, featured Steve as lead guitarist on virtually every song, and his solos on Ain't Nobody Lonely, Last Night I Wrote A Song, and Electric Guitar are some of the best moments on the entire album.

In the summer of 2016, Steve and I did our first official duo EP called Cary and Steve, A Couple of Guitar Players Sittin' around Pickin' featuring some guitar instrumentals that showcase the incredible talent of my longtime friend. It also marked Steve's first foray into songwriting, as he and I co-wrote the title song Sittin around Picking. The EP also features our single, Sounds Like Texas, that was featured in the summer 2016 Compilation CD produced by Texas Music Magazine. The title cut for Sittin' around Pickin' is featured on the Lubbock Music Now 2017 Compilation CD that features Steve and me, and eighteen other West Texas artists and songwriters.

Steve and I are featured as "real life" musicians/characters in the late Johnny Hughes 2016 fiction novel, "A Texas Beauty, Smart and Strong." I'm still trying to wrap my head around the bizarre literary concept of being a real life person in a fictional novel.

Steve has experienced some unbelievable bad luck and trouble in his life, but has demonstrated his unmovable faith and indomitable spirit by remaining a creative, caring, and loving man who has taken the despair and soul-sadness and channeled it into beautiful and inspired music.

Since that day in 1965, Steve Williams has been my all-time favorite guitar player.

FIFTEEN SECONDS OF FILM FAME

Back in the mid-1960's, Modern artist/filmmaker Andy Warhol made the statement that "in the future, everyone will be famous for 15 minutes." Reality TV and the internet have proven Andy to be a remarkably insightful prophet. I suppose every musician dreams of being a movie actor, and every actor wants to be a singer, and every songwriter wants to have his songs featured in films and TV. My 15/1000th of a second of film fame came courtesy of my friend and former student, Jeremy Boreing.

Jeremy had been living in L.A. and working in the TV and film business for several years when he decided to write, direct, and produce his own movie. In the hot, dry summer of 2012, he journeyed home, and with his friend, Johnathan Hay, wrote and shot the independent film, The Arroyo. The movie was filmed entirely on location in and around Slaton, Texas, using all-local actors, crew, and staging. Local musicians and entertainers, Kenny Maines and Junior Vasquez, and local actors, Glen Polk and David Armendariz, were cast in the lead roles.

Jeremy related the basic plot of the movie to me, which inspired me to write a Spanish-flavored guitar instrumental to submit as a possible theme or as underscore music. Unfortunately, he was unable to find a spot in the film where my instrumental fit, so it wasn't included. However, Jeremy assembled as many family, friends, neighbors as he could to be part of the large crowd scene in the final frames. At the very end, if you look closely and don't blink, you might catch a glimpse of my hat.

A couple of interesting quotes came out of the local movie-making experience. Arroyo writer and director, Jeremy Boreing, quipped, "Directing is like painting, except that all your colors have choices." Leading man, Kenny Maines, was quoted as saying, "Acting is easier than real life because you always know what you're going to say."

I've also had some "almost like a professional" success in the television world. As part of The Maines Brothers Band I had the honor of performing on the iconic Austin City Limits TV show, as well as Nashville Now, New Country, and The Texas Connection on the Nashville Network and the CBS Evening News. In 2005, I was interviewed about my relationship with Natalie Maines and the Dixie Chicks on the Entertainment Cable Network program E! True Hollywood Story: Country Divas.

As featured artist and co-host with Kenny Maines, I won a Silver Telly Video award for the Public Television series, Story Tellers and Music Makers. It was produced and directed by Doug Nelson and Tom Stalcup, and filmed entirely on location in the Tom T. Hall Production Studio in the Creative Arts building at South Plains College.

Of course, these days a cup of coffee at most establishments requires you to take out a second mortgage on your home.

As my dad would so eloquently say, "All that . . . and a dollar will get you a cup of coffee." Of course, these days a cup of coffee at most establishments requires you to take out a second mortgage on your home.

My dad had his own fifteen seconds of film fame, however, on the Midnight Cowboy movie. Some parts were filmed in and around Big Spring, Texas, and the production company used a couple of his antique cars in some scenes. The award-winning movie, starring Jon Voight and Dustin Hoffman, was quite controversial at the time, and was the only X-rated movie to ever win an academy award. My dad was not aware of the nature of the film when he leased his cars, and was not all that pleased that they had been used in some pretty racy scenes. But he did cash the check.

OPENING ACT

For all of us musician/performers who have been the opening act for a major superstar, has-been, or up-and-coming young star, we realize that at best we are considered the second-class citizens of the entertainment world. We understand the crowd is there to hear the headliner, and we're what is known as "value added." We are mostly there to fill some time and make the crowd feel like they're getting their money's worth. If we're lucky, the headliner actually hears part of our set, and on some happy occasions, actually takes the time to let us know they like what we're doing.

For all of us musician/performers who have been the opening act for a major superstar, has-been, or up-and-coming young star, we realize that at best we are considered the second-class citizens of the entertainment world.

Over the years, with the many bands I've worked with, I've had the great privilege to be the opening act for such great artists as Barbara Mandrell, Ronnie Milsap, Alabama, Dottie West, B. J. Thomas, Charlie Pride, Gary Stewart, Asleep at the Wheel, Tanya Tucker, and others. 99% of these wonderful artists are warm, accommodating, down-to-earth folks who remember they were once the opening act. But then there's the other 1%.

One particular incident stands out, when I was working with my good friend, "Honest" Rex Thomas and the Rex Thomas Band, aka the "Rex Thomas Stringed Orchestra." We were performing as part of the Texas Tech Raider Alley music, food, and family fun festivities, held prior to Texas Tech home football games. The Raider Alley originally featured local West Texas bands and acts, but as the events became more successful, major touring acts were added. The Rex Thomas Band was scheduled to open the show for an up-and-coming "Nashville Star," who had a couple of chart hits. For the sake of the anonymity, I'll refer to him as Mr. Big Shot. Because of television coverage, this particular Saturday game had a noon start-time. Consequently, we were told to show up for a 9 a.m. sound check.

When we arrived, Mr. Big Shot was already there, in the middle of what turned out to be a long and exasperating sound check. We stood around and patiently waited . . . and waited . . . and waited. Finally, it was about ten minutes before we were scheduled to start playing, and we hadn't even had a chance to put our equipment on stage, much less do our own sound check.

At last, when Mr. Big Shot left the stage and his band was still sound checking, Rex had had enough and simply proceeded to move the headliner's equipment out of the way so he could set up his amp.

Taking great offense, the bass player said, "Keep your hands off my gear."

To which Rex replied, "We're about to start our set, and I'm getting my gear in place."

The bass player got in Rex's face. "Take your hands off my stuff, or I'm going straight to the bus and get Mr. Big Shot."

Rex looked him straight in the eye and said, "You go get Mr. Big Shot and tell him to come on up on stage, and I'll stomp a mudhole right in the middle of his ass."

Our drummer, Jeff Hammond, and I just looked at each other thinking, Did Rex just say what I thought he said?"

The incensed bass player immediately ran to the promoter to complain. The promoter, who was a longtime friend of Rex's, simply shrugged his shoulders and assured the guy that Rex could and would, indeed, "stomp a mudhole in the guy's ass." Laughing at Rex's comment, we quickly set up our gear and played our always-fun and high-energy set. Mr. Big Shot and his band took the stage right after us and played a good set, and the bass player never said a word or made eye contact with Rex.

GEAR HEADS

My grandad, William Russell Banks Sr., was a carpenter. During the Great Depression, he worked on President Roosevelt's Works Project Administration (WPA) and helped build the Big Spring, Texas amphitheater and the city's municipal golf course. He had a little workshop out behind his house, and we kids loved to watch him work. Sometimes he would let us use the big table saw and some of his other tools. My younger brothers, Russ and Jake, would follow grandad around like a couple of little puppies.

My dad was a genius in spatial thinking and using his hands. He was a mechanic and restorer of antique cars. He built his first home and drew up blueprints for his ten-thousand square foot shop that he and my two younger brothers built in Sand Springs, Texas. It's not much of an exaggeration to say that my dad could overhaul a car on the side of the road using only a screw driver, a pair of pliers, and a crescent wrench. It was almost as though he could just wave his hand over a faulty engine and it would immediately start running. All of us boys grew up in his mechanic shops, and I put in many an hour cleaning parts in a naphtha bath, grinding valves on a wire-brush grinder, and cleaning up the shop with sawdust floor sweep. I learned to do basic car maintenance, like changing spark plugs, replacing water pumps, and changing oil and transmission fluid, but unlike my two brothers, I did not inherit any of the family mechanical aptitude. In fact, to this day I would rather take a beating than work on an automobile. I hated bustin' my knuckles, and I doubt I could even find the water pump on any of today's engines. My brother, Russ, took over my dad's antique car business when he passed.

> *I hated bustin' my knuckles, and I doubt I could even find the water pump on any of today's engines.*

From a young age, my brother, Jake, showed signs of genius in spatial thinking and working with his hands. He is a master builder and remodeler, and watching him hang drywall is like watching a famous artist paint a masterpiece. My favorite quote from him is, "A lot of great inventions were made by someone trying to figure out a way to dodge work." My life and my job as a piano player have been immensely blessed by some genius technicians who figured out a way to make a digital piano sound and feel like a real piano, while still being light enough for just about anyone to pick up and haul around.

Working in music stores, I learned some basic skills of instrument repair, wire soldering, and guitar maintenance and adjustment, but I was never what you would call a gear head. I learned the terms, the brands, and the function of music gear, but I was never immersed in knowing every nuance of signal flow, compression rate, and all that goes with being an expert technician. As the late, great Gary Stewart would say, "I just pick." However, I have the upmost respect for live sound engineers, studio recording engineers, master luthiers, amp repairmen, and all the other folks that make my performing possible.

I have had the honor and good fortune to work with some of the best live sound tech guys in the business, including Joe Piland, Matt Quick, and Jeremiah Denning, just to name a few. I've also had the privilege of working with some of the best studio engineers, including Don Caldwell, Lloyd Maines, Norman Petty, Jerry Kennedy, Lou Bradley, Scott Faris, Alan Crossland, Dolf Guardiola, Wally Moyers, Brent King, Bill VornDick, Mark Murray, Stuart Moody, Amy Devoge, and Justin Robinett. I also have the upmost respect and trust for master luthiers and instrument repairmen such as John McDonald and Dr. Jerry Goolsby, and piano technicians and tuners like my friend, Byron Nicholson.

Over the many years, I have discovered that all the great technical folks I've worked with have an absolute commitment to make the musical performer sound as good as they possibly can. They also have a deep, abiding respect for the audience they are serving, and try their very best to make sure the listener has the best sonic experience possible. While I may not be a gear head, I do understand that the men and women behind the sound board make possible everything I do up on the stage. I am in awe of the knowledge, the expertise, the professionalism, and the true love of the art and science of sound demonstrated by these professional gear heads.

OLD GUY ROCK

As the great baseball pitcher, Satchel Paige, once said, "Age is just mind over matter. If you don't mind, it don't matter." He proved that by pitching in professional baseball until he was over fifty years old. Of course, getting older comes with its own set of obstacles. They say when you reach a certain age, everything hurts . . . and what don't hurt . . . don't work. My friend, singer-songwriter, author and playwright, Andy Wilkinson, once famously opined, "You know you're getting old in the music business when at the end of the night you're much more interested in finding a roadie that a groupie."

My grandkids have become quite fond of reminding me of my senior citizen status.

A couple of years ago, when my granddaughter, Paisely, was six years old, she matter-of-factly stated, "PaPa, you're like really, really old. Well, not old dead, but really, really old." I felt only slightly better when, while playing tag with my grandson, Jaxon, who was eight at the time, he looked around as I was chasing him and remarked, "Wow, PaPa, you're faster than you look."

Despite my grandkids' assessment of my age, I've been getting paid to play music for over fifty years now, and I'm amazed and grateful to still

The Legendary Song Jammers
Tribute to Marty Robbins
"EL PASO" • "BIG IRON" • "DEVIL WOMAN" • "RIBBON OF DARKNESS"

The Legendary Song Jammers:
Curtis McBride • Jerry Brownlow • Steve Williams • Cary C. Banks

Photo courtesy - Sydney Cox

be a performing singer/songwriter/musician after all these years. I'm truly blessed to be in a business where, if you're willing, you can keep on working as long as your body will let you.

I feel eternally blessed to still be playing and enjoying being onstage, and having a great time playing music. A while back, my buddies, Jerry Brownlow, Steve Williams, Curtis McBride, and I were playing a family-friendly gig where folks ages two to ninety-two were present. On one of our breaks, a young boy, who looked to be about nine years old, approached and excitedly engaged me in a lively discussion.

Boy: "Your band is awesome, mister. How long have you been playing music?"

Me: "Since way before your parents were even born."

Boy: "That's a long time. How old are you really?"

Me: "Sixty-seven."

Boy: "Wow! You're older than my grandpa . . . and you're still rockin'."

I don't think I've ever enjoyed, or appreciated, a compliment as much.

Les Paul was playing jazz gigs in downtown Manhattan well into his nineties; Willie Nelson and Kris Kristofferson are still on the road; Mick Jagger, Keith Richards, and Paul McCartney are still headlining worldwide tours. And me . . . well, I wrote this song:

Old Guy Rock
Words & Music Cary C. Banks

V1)
Well I used to be a lean mean rockin' machine
Way back in high school
Had a little band called the Psychedelic Figs
Man, we thought we was cool
We played the Beatles, the Stones, the Kinks, and the Who
Chuck Berry and the Dave Clark Five
We never realized, the way time flies
You turn around and 40 years have gone by
Now the hairs gettin' thinner, the middle's getting thicker
Mylanta is the drug of choice
Our GTO's are Now SUV's,
But man we can still make noise

Chorus)
We're playin' Old Guy Rock, yeah Old Guy Rock
Give me the beat boys is sweeter as the years go by
Well I may be over the hill but that's all right
I'm playin' Old Guy Rock
Rockin' till the day I die

V2)
Now my son's got his own little rock and roll band
And they sure draw a crowd
Some kind of heavy metal somethin' or other
They're good but man they're loud
Sometimes they ask me to sing 'em a song
Or show 'em a Hendrix riff
I tell 'em 'bout Woodstock and 8-track tapes
They laugh at what we once called hip
They've got the tattoos, the earrings, the glitz, and the glam

Like the stars on the MTV
But they don't realize, the way time flies
And just how soon "they'll be"

Chorus)
Playin' Old Guy Rock, yeah Old Guy Rock
Give me the beat boys is sweeter as the years go by
Well I may be over the hill , but that's all right
I'll be rockin' and rollin' down the other side

©2009 CC Writer Music ASCAP

HARD COUNTRY, GREAT MUSIC

Many people, especially those not from Texas, have often asked me, "What is this Texas Music scene all about, and more specifically, how do you explain all this great music that has come out of this flat, dry land of West Texas?"

The name Texas originally came from the Hasini Native American Indian word, Tejas, which means "friends." The land is as vast and multi-dimensional as the music that has emanated from it since the earliest times. From the nomadic Native American tribes, to Spanish explorers, to the early settlers, we have always been a fiercely independent people, regardless of race or place of origin. We are the only state in the United States to have once been a sovereign nation.

The area of West Texas has a geographic reach that, debatably, stretches as far north as Amarillo, as far east as Abilene, as far west as the New Mexico state line and El Paso, and as far south as Wink, Pecos, and San Angelo. Most of what is referred to as West Texas is flat, dry, and windblown. It's been called cotton country, the oil patch, beef land, and the southern tip of the Dust Bowl. Generations of family farms and ranches, small towns, family-owned businesses, and small churches have defined the people and the land. It's hard country, and the people are hardworking, hard living, hard partying, and hard praying. Driving through this vast stretch of land, the nose is assaulted with the choking dust from cotton gins, the noxious odor of the cattle feedlots, and the gassy smell of pumpjacks and oil refineries, all of which the old timers will proudly affirm "smells like money."

From Bob Wills and Buddy Holly, to Natalie Maines and David Gashen, this patch of hard country has produced some of the most revered and influential music makers the world has ever known. The answer to the question of why this area has produced so many great musicians, songwriters, and artists has been pondered by many. West Texas legendary artist and songwriter, Joe Ely, once famously answered with, "There's nothin' else to do."

From the old-time barn dances, to the tiny churches, to the honky-tonks and bars, Texas musicians and songwriters have combined the heart of every style of music from just about every area of the world to make this wonderful stew we call Texas Music. These days, we have our own music charts, our own television and radio shows, and our music business that supports a large number of artists, venues, and styles: rock and roll, country, R&B, bluegrass, Tejano, Roots Americana, and good ol' Western Swing. And it all Sounds Like Texas to Me. *

In my opinion, the answer to why all this great music has come out of West Texas is the heart of West Texas: the family.

*Sounds Like Texas © 2016 Cary C. Banks/Bankonit Music LLC

> From the old-time barn dances, to the tiny churches, to the honky-tonks and bars, Texas musicians and songwriters have combined the heart of every style of music from just about every area of the world to make this wonderful stew we call Texas Music.

IT'S A FAMILY AFFAIR

Life's a song, we're all singin'
Life's a song that never ends
Pass it on to sons and daughters
And it starts all over again

©*John Hadley, Hadley Six Music BMI, Admin: Sony ATV BMI*

I have been blessed to work onstage and in the recording studio with some of the finest people on the face of God's green earth. I've also had the unique experience of witnessing first-hand the gift of family musical talent handed down from generation to generation. It is truly amazing how impactful and far- reaching is the musical legacy of a handful of West Texas families.

MAINES FAMILY

As a member of The Maines Brothers Band, I've had the honor of working with brothers Lloyd, Steve, Kenny, and Donnie Maines; and their sister, LaTronda Moyers. Their dad, James Maines, and his brothers, Wayne, Don, and Uncle Son, were the original Maines Brothers Band that performed around the West Texas area in the 1950's and '60's. As youngsters, Kenny, Lloyd, and Steve would perform as The Little Maines Brothers Band. In the late '70's, Donnie joined the band, and with fiddler, Richard Bowden, and brothers, Randy and Jerry Brownlow, began performing and recording as The Maines Brothers Band. In 1983, when Randy Brownlow left the band, I joined as keyboard player. In 1993, as a music instructor at South Plains College, Lloyd's youngest daughter, Natalie, was one of my students. Of course, the incredible success of Natalie with the Dixie Chicks has become the stuff of legends. A few years after Natalie left South Plains College, her cousins, Chad and Casey Maines, Donnie's sons, were both students there. Chad has gone on to play drums with several famous acts, including the Texas Playboys. Casey has played guitar with a number of well-known performers,

The Maines Brothers Band on stage with kids and grandkids during 50th year Celebration Concert
Photo courtesy- Rick Vanderpool

including the Hogg Maulies. Kenny's son, Brian, has performed in musical productions at the Cactus Theater, written songs, and recorded with his dad, and leads the Paradigm Worship Team at First Baptist Church in Lubbock. The fourth generation of Maines family performers are now appearing on the scene with Kim Maines Maguire's daughter, Amelia, and Natalie Maines' son, Slade Pasdar, displaying tremendous talent as singer/songwriter/musicians.

CALDWELL FAMILY

Don Caldwell has been a tremendous part of the West Texas music and entertainment scene for decades as a gifted saxophonist, recording engineer, record producer, concert promoter, and venue owner. His wife, Terri Sue, is a tremendous vocalist, songwriter, and music teacher who had a Top 40 hit several years ago called Gypsy Eyes. Don and Terri's children, Todd, Cami, and Toby, are all talented former students of South Plains College. Todd, an incredible keyboardist, has recorded and performed with such iconic stars as Crosby, Stills and Nash, Bonnie

Raitt, Kashmere and Burlap, and has composed soundtrack music for the Joel David Moore film, Spiral. Cami, vocalist and actress, has performed countless comedy, drama, and musical theater productions, and continues to produce and guide the careers of young talent such as the Cactus Cuties of Lubbock. Toby has performed as sound engineer/producer at Caldwell recording studios, and as drummer and band leader of the Cactus Theater. Now living in Nashville, he has worked with many well-known artists, including Leon Russell. Over the years, I've had the wonderful experience of performing onstage with all the members of the Caldwell family.

MOYERS FAMILY

Wally Moyers Jr. has been a mainstay in the West Texas music scene for many years. His dad, Wally Sr., played steel guitar for a number of artists, including Waylon Jennings, Bill Mack, Slim Whitman, Tommy Hancock, and many others. Shortly before his death, I had the opportunity to perform with Wally Sr. on the West Texas Opry. He passed on his love and talent for the pedal steel guitar to his son, Wally Jr., who has worked and recorded with such well-known artists as Terry McBride, Hank Thompson, Johnny Duncan, John Conley, Jimmie Dale Gilmore, Teea Goins, Larry Gatlin, Michael Martin Murphy, and a host of others. As a recording engineer and owner of Studio 84, Wally Jr. has worked with such iconic artists as Delbert McClinton, Terry McBride, Don Wise, Richie McDonald, Marcia Ball, Bobby Keys, Christyana Perez and Megan Laurie, and Jerry Brownlow. Wally and I have performed together in the Rex Thomas Band and in Wally and the Gators. He has passed along his love and talent for the steel guitar to his son, Jeremy, who was a student at South Plains College as well. Jeremy left college to join his buddy, Richie McDonald, in the award-winning band, Lonestar. Jeremy and I have performed together at South Plains College and with Richie McDonald and the Rex Thomas Band. Wally's son, Swade, also attended South Plains College, and with brother Jeremy, directs the operations of the Moyers Group, which includes designing and installing Audio/Video/Lighting systems across the country. Wally and LaTronda's sons,

Brady and Breck, both saxophonists and guitarist, have also recorded songs with their dad. Jeremy Moyers' sons, trumpeter, Haydn, and guitarist and saxophonist, Clay, are the fourth generation of Moyers family musicians bitten by the music bug. They are already sought-after performers in their school and church bands. Another fourth generation musician, Wally Moyers Sr.'s great-grandson, Logan Brodus, currently tours with the Randall King Band, playing guitar and pedal steel.

HANCOCK FAMILY

During the 1950's and 60's, Tommy and Charlene Hancock were mainstays in the West Texas Music scene. Tommy's band, The Roadside Playboys, was one of the most sought-after dance bands in the region, featuring Tommy on guitar and vocals, Dick Barnett on drums, Curly Lawler on fiddle, Bob Stufflebeme on steel guitar, and a host of other West Texas musicians. After Tommy saw a beautiful young vocalist and guitar player named Charlene on the Circle 13 Ranch TV show, he hired her in his band and eventually married her. In the 1970's, Tommy and Charlene moved to New Mexico and formed Tommy X and the Supernatural Family Band with daughters, Traci and Conni, and son, Jaquin. After Tommy retired from the music business, Charlene, Traci, and Conni formed the iconic Texana Dames. Daughter Holi married a young drummer from Lubbock named Richard Barnett, the son of Roadside Playboys drummer, Dick Barnett. I had the delightful pleasure of performing with the Texana Dames back in the early 1990's.

BLAKELY FAMILY

In 1968, recording artists and performers, Jimmy and Dorothy Blakely, moved from Roswell, New Mexico to West Texas and purchased the Palm Room Nightclub on the Idalou Highway, east of Lubbock. The Palm Room became a legendary performance venue that featured both national touring acts and local acts, including Jimmy's Band, which featured Jimmy on fiddle and Dorothy on piano and string bass. Over the years many local musicians performed in the Palm Room band, including Steve Maines, who played bass with the group. The Palm Room also featured an indoor pool and Tiki room that would become a favorite venue for Texas Tech fraternity and sorority parties, featuring countless local rock and country bands. As Jimmy and Dorothy's children grew, they also became members of the band: Jimmy Lee played fiddle, Ronnie sang and played guitar, steel guitar, and banjo; daughter Debbie sang, wrote songs, and played piano. Jimmy Jr. and Debbie and her husband, Charlie Eaton, performed with groups such as Warhorse, and the Planets. Ron moved to Nashville, where he worked with several recording acts, including Darron Norwood. Ron now has a music ministry in Nashville with his wife and sons Josh, Wes, Ben, and daughter-in-law, Anna. Ron's son, Ben, is now the third-generation pedal steel guitarist in the Blakely family music legacy. Debbie and her husband, Charlie, now reside in Lubbock. Charlie is employed at Moyers Sound Solutions.

VASQUEZ/STUFFLEBEME FAMILY

In the early 1970's, while still a student at Lubbock High School, Calistro "Junior" Vasquez and his buddies, the Tennequeye brothers, formed the folk rock band, Peyote. The group was highly successful in the West Texas area and traveled around the state of Texas. Also during his time at Lubbock High school, Junior met a young lady named Mickie Stufflebeme, the piano accompanist for the school choir. Mickie's father, Bob Stufflebeme, had been a professional musician in the Lubbock area in the 1950's and 60's, and had played steel guitar with Tommy Hancock and the Roadside Playboys. Bob had also been part of a band accompanying a young Elvis Presley when he performed at the legendary Cotton Club in Lubbock. After Bob retired from performing, he owned his own tool business, and as a side business, designed and built his own pedal steel guitars. (One of his earliest customers was a young steel guitarist from Lubbock, Lloyd Maines.) Junior Vasquez and Mickie Stufflebeme were married in the late 1970's, and performed as a duo and with various bands. In the early 1980's, when Junior and Mickie had their children Mikeala, Micah, and Victoria, they left the secular music scene and began a music ministry. The Vasquez family music ministry has blessed several churches in the Lubbock area, and in 2011 Junior and Mickie, along with some close friends, established the Gathering at Spirit Ranch church. Junior is also a very successful local performer and jingle writer. Mickie taught voice at the South Plains College Commercial Music program and now teaches voice at Caldwell studios. Micah is a professional bass player who has worked with several well-known acts, including Bart Crow and Kirk Braxley. Victoria "Tori" has become an award-winning singer songwriter and has traveled with such well-known acts as Blue October. She performs with her husband, Shannon, in the Battling Nelsons Band.

BROWNLOW FAMILY

Edward Lee Brownlow and wife, Jerri, owned a family farm near Morton, Texas in the 1950's and 60's, and with sons, Randy and Jerry Dale, created the Brownlow Family Band. Jerri had been a successful singer and guitarist in the 1950's, and had turned down a recording contract with a national label to stay in West Texas and raise her two young sons. The Brownlow Family Band featured Edward, who played the mandolin and harmonica, and Jerri, who played guitar and sang. Young Randy played piano, guitar, banjo, and fiddle, and Jerry Dale played the bass and rhythm guitar. The band was managed by legendary West Texas radio personality William "High Pockets" Duncan. The Brownlow Family Band created and hosted a monthly country music Opry-style show in Morton, Texas, that showcased West Texas talent, including a young red-haired girl named Terri Sue Newman. Years later with her husband, Don Caldwell, Terri Sue would own and operate the famous Cactus Theater in Lubbock. Randy and Jerry would go on to successful careers in the music business as members of the Maines Brothers Band, performing with many well-known artists.

Other West Texas musical families I've had the privilege to perform with include:

CORBIN FAMILY

Clois Ray "Slim" Corbin and brother, Glen "Sky" Corbin, bought KLLL Radio in 1958, and hired young Waylon Jennings as an on-air D J. Ray, Waylon, and Buddy Holly made a rough demo of Buddy's song, You're The One, in the small KLLL production studio. Waylon and Ray were given writing credit on the song as well. Later, Ray "Slim" sold his interest in KLLL radio and moved to Arizona, where he became a songwriter and recording artist with Monument and Columbia Records. His song, Come on Home and Sing the Blues for Daddy, was recorded by several artists, including Waylon Jennings, and became a Top 10 hit for Bob Luman. Ray's son, Michael, is a singer/guitarist who has worked with several West Texas bands, including Rat Madness, The Jack Bowden Band, Maverick, Riverwind, The Caprockers, and the Penni Lawrence Band. Michael also worked for several years as on-air radio personality at KLLL, KFMX, and 98Kool radio stations in Lubbock. I've had the privilege to work onstage with Michael several times.

GLEN FAMILY

In the 1950' and 60's, a popular West Texas group was Mac Glenn and the Roadside Ramblers. Mac's brother, Artie, played and recorded with legendary groups like The Light Crust Doughboys, Bob Wills, and Lefty Frizzel. Artie was an accomplished songwriter and his song, Crying in the Chapel, was a big hit for Elvis Presley. When Mac's son, Royce, was just fifteen, he joined his dad's band. At seventeen, Royce hit the road, playing with Larry Trider and the Road Riders. Throughout his long career, Royce has traveled all over the country, performing and recording with such well-known artists as John Conlee, Bo Diddley, Waylon Jennings, Sammi Smith, Steve Wariner, The Maines Brothers Band, Joe Ely, and countless others. I've had the privilege to perform with Royce as part of Bo Diddley's backup band, Joey Allen, the Almost Live Band, and the Rex Thomas Band. Royce's son, Dustin, is a talented singer and songwriter as well.

BOWDEN FAMILY

As a member of The Maines Brothers Band, The Panhandle Mystery Band, and the West Texas Opry Stage Band, I've been privileged to work with legendary fiddler, Richard Bowden. I've also had the honor to work with Richard's brother, Jack, who is a talented multi-instrumentalist and music teacher. Their dad, Bert Bowden, was a college professor who was a professional entertainer in his younger days. He recorded some songs for Bethlehem records such as Burned in Carolina (as Bert Bryson and his Musical Boys). Although all of Bert's kids are musicians and singers, those who have been seriously pursuing music as a career are: Richard Bowden, Jack Bryson Bowden, Joyce Leigh Bowden, and the younger sisters, Kristen Rae Bowden and Amy Lilani Bowden.

HARTIN FAMILY

As a member of the faculty, I had the privilege to work musically, both academically and professionally, with John Hartin; guitarist, educator, entrepreneur, and original Chairman of the Creative Arts Department at South Plains College. John's son, Gordon, has performed as steel guitarist for Shooter Jennings band, and John's youngest son, Chester, was keyboard player in the South Plains Opry ensemble class I directed at South Plains College.

LAWSON/CLANTON FAMILY

Singer, Liz Lawson Clanton, and I have played gigs together in the Don Caldwell band, and she recorded my song, Here I Am on the Radio, on Texas Soul Records. Her daughter, Kristi Clanton, and I performed together in a show produced by the Cactus Theater.

MARTINEZ FAMILY

Guitarist Luis Martinez and I performed together in the Jazz Alley band. His son, Vince, and I have performed as a duo and in his band, The Tritones.

ALLEN FAMILY

As part of their Panhandle Mystery Band, I have performed onstage and on recordings with artist songwriter, Terry Allen. His son, Bukka, (piano and accordion) has worked with well-known artists such as Ian Moore. Bukka and his younger brother, Bale, (drums) have performed with Terry on Austin City Limits and participated in mammoth jams of the Panhandle Mystery Band.

SALDANA FAMILY

I have performed several country dances with vocalist and bass player, Alfred Saldana. His son, Jay, was a student of mine at South Plains College, and has also drummed for Texas country artists, Wade Bowen and Williams Clark Green, and the Rex Thomas Band.

JAMES FAMILY

Western Swing musicians, Buzz James (fiddler) and his wife, Jewette James (piano), were members of John Lee Wills Band (Bob Wills Brother) in the 1950's and 60's. I was privileged to play several gigs with them and learned a great deal about swing and stride piano style from Jewette. Their son, Johnny, was my bandmate in the Free Whiskey Band. Their daughter, Dr. Rebecca Chapel, a talented musician as well, is a respected Professor of Music at Anderson University, where she has been an integral part of the University's Music Business Program.

GREEN FAMILY

I have had the privilege of performing both church and secular gigs with music ministers, Tom and Sherry Green, and their sons, Rocky and Caleb, who were both students at South Plains College.

RICHARDSON FAMILY

Johnny Richardson, a popular West Texas singer/guitarist, and I have shared the stage a time or two. His son, Cale, an award-winning student at South Plains College, plays guitar and keyboard with the Eli Young

Band. Cale and my son, Cody, played together in the Honeybrowne Band and Ryan James band.

NIX FAMILY

I once had the honor of auditioning for legendary Western Swing artist, Hoyle Nix. His son, Jody, and I played together in the Coahoma High School Band.

TURPIN FAMILY

As a member of the West Texas Opry Stage Band, I had the privilege of performing with legendary western swing fiddler, Weldon Turpin, and his son, Ricky, who have performed with such well-known bands as Asleep at the Wheel.

NEWTON FAMILY

Drummer, David Newton, and I did a couple of gigs in the early 1980's with singer Eileen Durham (Aikin). David's son, Jason, was a student of mine at South Plains College, and he and I have done some professional gigs together as well.

GARRETT FAMILY

Guitarist and artist, Dustin Garrett, was a student of mine at South Plains College, and has worked as the musical director at the Cactus Theater in Lubbock. Dustin and I worked several gigs together, including with Australian artist, Megan Laurie. Dustin's dad, Mike, also an artist, worked for several years as stage manager at the Cactus Theater. Dustin's wife, Kristi, was one of my students at South Plains College, and she and I have worked together with Megan Laurie as well.

PADEN FAMILY

Mark Paden is a talented singer/songwriter/musician, whose original songs have been recorded by such artists as The Maines Brothers Band, T. G. Shepherd, John Conlee, The Kendalls, and others. Mark has been a mainstay at the Cactus Theater in Lubbock for years, and was part of the legendary vocal group The JD's. Mark's daughter, Cathy, is a talented vocalist, who performs with her husband, Ken Lince, who was once part of the group, Laredo. Ken and Cathy are often joined by drummer, Michael, "Lefty" Lefkowitz, who is married to Mark's younger daughter, Amy.

ON STAGE

I have been so blessed to have the opportunity to perform on stage with incredibly talented, graciously humble artists and musicians, including nationally and internationally known superstars as well as well known and respected Texas artists.

Performing on Thursday Nite Live TV Broadcast on the Tom T. Hall Stage, Cary Banks, Jedd Hughes, April Richards Hyde
Photo courtesy - Dan English/South Plaines College

South Plains College beauties Amanda Brown, Amber Pennington, Allison Branch, Shelley Lee performing on the South Plains Opry Show Mobile stage, Downtown Levelland Texas
Photo courtesy - Dan English/South Plains College

With Grammy winning songwriter/artists Terri Hendrix and Lloyd Maines on the Tom T Hall stage with South Plains College students Penny and Katy Clark and Preston Wait
Photo courtesy - Wes Underwood/South Plains College

With Lonestar's Richie McDonald at Cattle Barron's Ball, with SPC colleagues Wade McNutt, Bethany Borba and Mickie Vasquez
Photo courtesy - Wes Underwood/South Plains College

John Hartin and Cary Banks picking with South Plains College students, Jason Newton, Richie Dorman, Jeremy Robbins
Photo courtesy - Dan English/South Plains College

With guitar legends Lloyd Maines and Jesse Taylor
Stubbs Jam
Photo courtesy - TG Caraway Collection/ Southwest Collection/Special Collections Library/ Texas Tech University, Lubbock, Texas

Just a few of the other well known artists and musicians I've had the honor to "pick" with on stage include:

Natalie Maines and the Dixie Chicks, Tom T Hall, Johnny Hiland, Lucinda Williams, David Grissom, Pat Green, Johnny Gimble, Ponty Bone, Jimmie Dale Gilmore, Doug Smith, Sonny Curtis, Trent Wilmon, Heath Wright, Box Car Willie, Radney Foster, Jerrod Neiman, Charla Corn, Stoney LaRue, Chris Wall, Donnie Allison, Brad Leali, Tommy Allsup, Jason Wyatt, Clare Dunn, Megan Laurie, Connie Hanson, Jana Stanfield, Andy Wilkinson, Amanda Shires, Kevin Welch, John Hadley, Bob Livingston, Chuck Pyle, Hannah Jackson, Steve Meador, as well as the many other musicians and artists mentioned previously in the book.

BACKSTAGE

Here are some wonderful moments in my career captured off stage and backstage.

The Maines Brothers Band backstage with Country Music superstar, Barbara Mandrell
Photo courtesy - Maines Brothers Collection

Members of the Maines Brothers band and crew backstage with fiddle legend, Johnny Gimble
Photo courtesy - TG Caraway Collection/ Southwest Collection/Special Collections Library/Texas Tech University, Lubbock, Texas

Cary Banks being interviewed by legendary journalist and radio personality, Tumbleweed Smith
Photo courtesy - Rick Vanderpool

The Maines Brothers Band with Jerry Jeff Walker and his two children, Jessie and Django, at the White House Press room in Washington DC. Twenty years after this photo was taken, my son would be playing drums in Django Walker's band.
Photo courtesy - T G Caraway Collection/Southwest Collection/Special Collections Library/
Texas Tech University, Lubbock, Texas

ENCORE

2019 marks my fifty-fourth year as a paid musical performer, and I celebrate this milestone by releasing this book and a twelve-song instrumental piano album titled simply, Piano. My longtime friend and musical partner, Steve "Gittar" Williams, and I continue to perform and record; and I continue to write songs.

Several years ago I was honored to be part of a small group that started a little church service called "The Gathering." Led by my longtime friend, Calistro "Junior" Vasquez, this little group of believers has been meeting at the Spirit Ranch in Escondido Canyon for several years now. Every Sunday morning we congregate in what is now E & J BBQ Restaurant to lift up one another with prayer and praise, and to share the Word of God. Our Gathering Band, which includes Junior and Mickie Vasquez, Kenny Maines, Mike Caraway, and me, speak to one another in psalms, hymns, and spiritual songs, singing and playing, and making music in our hearts to the Lord.

I am there virtually every time the doors are open and . . . I have a key.

Sometimes we sing this song I wrote that my beloved friend, Jerry Brownlow, recorded on his gospel album.

The Gathering Praise group, Mickie Vasquez, Junior Vasquez, Kenny Maines, Cary Banks, Mike Carraway
Photo courtesy - The Gathering of Lubbock

More Love (Than When I Came)

Verse I:
I saw a sign on a car today, you know it made me grin
The words on the sign said, "Whoever dies with the most toys wins"
I recall a wise man said, "All is vain under the sun"
What will be the measure, when the race of life is run?

Chorus:
Will I leave this world more love than when I came?
Will the sum of all my days, be blessing or be blame?
Will anybody smile, at the mention of my name?
Will I leave this world more love than when I came?

Verse II:
It seems the world's gone crazy, just chasing down the wind.
We're searching for some meaning, while looking past a friend.
We trade our time for money, and throw away our peace of mind.
We pile up stacks of shiny stuff, just to leave it all behind.

More Love (Than When I Came) © 2016 Cary C. Banks

ACKNOWLEDGEMENTS

I have so many wonderful family and friends to thank for their help in making this project happen. I apologize preemptively, as I am sure I will miss someone. Please know that for each and every one of you, I am eternally grateful. My wife, Carol, for love, devotion, encouragement, and gentle editing ideas. My brother, Russ Banks, for gathering and sharing Banks' family history; and for the countless nights when he sacrificed his time and his Ford Torino to drive my bandmates and me to gigs all over West Texas, helping us load and unload gear, then driving us back home at ungodly late hours. I'm pretty sure we bought his beer, but I don't recall if we ever paid him much, if anything at all. My brother, Jake, for a lifetime of love and devotion and encouragement, my sister, Toya, for a lifetime of encouragement and love, and for assisting my memory of story details. My precious mom, Doris Banks, for love, devotion, caring, prayers, and assistance with family history and more story details. And to my son, Cody Banks, for his ever-present encouragement and inspiration, and for being brave enough, or crazy enough, to choose to make a life and career as a professional musician.

My dear friend, singer songwriter Terri Hendrix, for being one of the most vocal encouragers, pushing me to undertake the writing of this book.

My very special thanks to my friend and gracious editor, Jerry Stoddard, aka James Stoddard, well known author, songwriter, sound engineer, and noted college professor. His work on the project has been more valuable than mere words could ever express.

My daughter, Professor Katherine Banks, for her valuable assistance in pre-editing, encouragement, and advice. Thanks also to her husband, Christian Diamond, for his help and encouragement, and for designing and creating my website, carycbanks.com.

A very special thanks to all who provided information, helping to jog my memory and adding important details that had slipped my mind: Mark Gillespie, for his encouragement and assistance in locating folks vital to some of the stories, Marvin Wright, for his assistance in remembering stories, dates, people, and details. Muchas gracias to Dwaine Thomas, Rex Thomas, Lloyd Maines, Kenny Maines, Steve Maines, Donnie Maines, Jerry Brownlow, John Sprott, Dr. Daniel Johnson, Floyd Brown, and Tiffany Banks for guiding and providing me with information for the stories. A very grateful thank you to Don Caldwell, Mickie Vasquez, Wally Moyers, Jeremy Moyers, Latronda Maines Moyers, Royce Glen, Charlene Hancock, Richard Barnett, Debbie Blakely-Eaton, Jerry Brownlow, Tina Maines, Kim Maines Maguire, Jack Bowden, and so many others for information on the myriad of families listed in It's A Family Affair.

My deepest gratitude and thanks are extended to all the photographers who provided decades worth of photos for the book: the T. G. Caraway Collection, Joe Piland, the Robert Hudnal Collection, Shonda

Crutchfield Photography, Wes Underwood and Dan English with South Plains College, Alice Smith, Scott Faris, the Maines Brothers Collection, Matt Barnes, the Lubbock Avalanche Journal, Greg Kreller, Chris Hudgins, Karen Jent Pollard, Paul Milosevich, Milton Adams, the Texas Music Office, the West Texas Music Association, the Academy of Country Music, ASCAP, and the Country Music Association.

Also, to Mark Hartsfield and Amanda Sneed at Hartsfield Design, Dr. Jerry Goolsby, Rick Vanderpool, Brian Atkinson, Suzanne Henley, Chris Hudgins, Floyd Brown, John Hadley, Curtis Peoples, Kyle Abernathie, Andy Wilkinson and so many others for encouragement and assistance in the technical aspects of putting this little tome together.

Other thanks must go to longtime friends and dedicated fans: Ann Powell, Lesli Shepherd, Mary Hall, Karen Jent, and countless others. For valuable literary advice, approval, and encouragement, I need to thank Rusty and Schahara Hudelson, Dennis Howard, Rick Vanderpool, Joe Nick Patoski, and Jeremy Boreing.

My dad would often quote King Solomon: "Let us hear the conclusion of the matter: Fear God and keep his commandments, for this is the whole duty of man." Ecclesiastes 12:13

That's my story and I'm stickin' to it.

Thank you for reading the book.

Blessings of peace, love, and happiness be with you always; and may you have music wherever you go.

Cary C. Banks